So...
you
think
you
know
the
Bible?

More Than 700 Questions to Test
Your Scripture Knowledge

D0802616

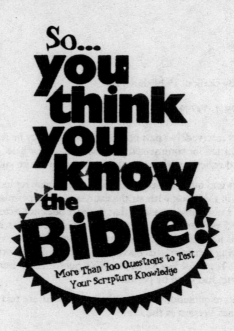

So... you think you know the Bible?

More Than 100 Questions to Test
Your Scripture Knowledge

CONOVER SWOFFORD

BARBOUR
PUBLISHING

Published by Barbour Publishing, Inc., P.O. Box 719, Uhrichsville, Ohio 44683, www.barbourbooks.com

Our mission is to publish and distribute inspirational products offering exceptional value and biblical encouragement to the masses.

Member of the
Evangelical Christian
Publishers Association

Printed in the United States of America.

5 4 3

Contents

Introduction 7
Quiz 1: Who's Who in the Old Testament. 9
Quiz 2: Relatives, Part 1 16
Quiz 3: Parables 23
Quiz 4: Places of Worship 30
Quiz 5: Meanings of Words, Part 1 37
Quiz 6: The Twelve Tribes 44
Quiz 7: The Holy Spirit 51
Quiz 8: Angels 58
Quiz 9: Priests. 65
Quiz 10: Prophecies 72
Quiz 11: Numbers 79
Quiz 12: Who's Who in the New Testament. . . . 86
Quiz 13: Occupations. 93
Quiz 14: God 100
Quiz 15: By Any Other Name 107
Quiz 16: Prophets. 114
Quiz 17: Royalty, Part 1 121
Quiz 18: Jesus. 128
Quiz 19: Geography 135
Quiz 20: Meanings of Words, Part 2 142
Quiz 21: Hodgepodge 149
Quiz 22: Animal, Vegetable, Mineral 156

Quiz 23:   References and Quotes 163
Quiz 24:   Judges. 170
Quiz 25:   Royalty, Part 2 177
Quiz 26:   Who's Who, Again 184
Quiz 27:   Relatives, Part 2 191
Quiz 28:   The Lord's Army 198
Quiz 29:   God's Law 205
Quiz 30:   We Dare You to Answer These! 212
Answers. 223

Introduction

So...you think you know the Bible? Good—there's no better book!

But the Bible covers a lot of ground: more than five dozen books, nearly 1,200 chapters, more than 31,000 verses, and some 780,000 words. Are you still feeling confident?

As you make your way through the thirty quizzes in this book—and the more than 700 tough questions—you can measure your smarts by keeping score. Answers are found at the back of the book.

Of course, knowing *about* the Bible and knowing the God who gave us His Word are two different things. As you read, keep in mind that the Bible is "quick, and powerful, and sharper than any two-edged sword, piercing even to the dividing asunder of soul and spirit, and of the joints and marrow, and is a discerner of the thoughts and intents of the heart" (Hebrews 4:12).

Don't just *know* the Bible—*live* it!

Quiz 1

Who's Who in the Old Testament

The stories of these famous people were put in the Bible for a purpose. How much do you know about them?

1. Which of Job's friends—Zophar, Eliphaz, Elihu, or Bildad—arrived last?

2. How long did Job sit and mourn silently?

3. Why were the children of Israel condemned to wander in the wilderness for forty years?

4. Who touched the ark of the covenant and died?

5. When God asked Adam, "Have you eaten from the tree which I commanded you not to eat from(NIV)?" whom did Adam blame for his sin?

So...
you
think
you
know
the
Bible?

• • • • • • • • • •
Total possible points: 500
Your score: _____

• • • • • • • • • • •

1. When Naaman was cured of his leprosy, to what liar was the leprosy given?

2. Who led the victory song after the Egyptians were drowned in the Red Sea?

3. Who, besides Moses, had rods that turned into serpents?

4. Whose name means "day star"?

5. Who killed two people at once with one spear?

• • • • • • • • • •

Total possible points: 1,000
Your score: _____

1. What two people had time altered for them?

2. What three things did God command Moses to do at the burning bush?

3. What happened to the Philistines who stole the ark of the covenant?

4. What was the name of the servant Abraham was going to make his heir before Isaac was born?

5. When told that his sons had been killed and the ark of the covenant had been taken, who fell over backwards and died of a broken neck?

• • • • • • • • • • •
Total possible points: 1,500
Your score: _____

400
points
each

• • • • • • • • • • •

1. Whom did Rahab marry, and whose mother was she?

2. Who set up the Ebenezer?

3. What bad man got his head nailed to the ground?

4. Who is described in the Bible as having weak eyes?

5. What king's description says he came "delicately"?

• • • • • • • • • • •

Total possible points: 2,000
Your score: _____

• • • • • • • • • • •

1. What man did God strike dead for refusing to help David?

2. What was the name of the idol that kept falling on its face in front of the ark of the covenant?

3. What did Heber's wife, Jael, do that made her famous?

4. What two Old Testament figures didn't die?

5. What law did Naomi invoke to convince Boaz to marry Ruth?

• • • • • • • • • • •

Total possible points: 2,500
Your score: _____

Quiz 1

. . . .

Who's Who in
the Old Testament

Total points for this quiz: 7,500
Your score for this quiz: _____

Answers on page 223.

Quiz 2

Relatives, Part 1

It has been said that you can choose your friends but not your relatives. Good, bad, or ugly describes many of the following. What do you know about them?

• • • • • • • • • •

1. Whose wife told him to curse God and die?

2. Who was Abram's father?

3. Which two of Aaron's sons were devoured by fire?

4. Who was Noah's great-grandfather?

5. How were Esther and Mordecai related?

• • • • • • • • • •

Total possible points: 500
Your score: _____

1. What famous spy was the uncle of Othniel?

2. Who was Jethro's son-in-law?

3. What king was Mephibosheth's grandfather?

4. What wicked pair took issue with the prophecies of Elijah?

5. Who were the sons of Zebedee?

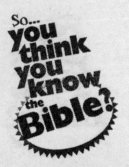

• • • • • • • • • • •
Total possible points: 1,000
Your score: _____

• • • • • • • • • • •

1. Who was Laban's brother-in-law?

2. What king claimed Ruth and Boaz as his great-grandparents?

3. What two men told foreign rulers that their wives were their sisters?

4. What good advice did Moses' father-in-law give him?

5. How was Joab, the commander of David's army, related to David?

• • • • • • • • • • •

Total possible points: 1,500
Your score: _____

1. Whose son was Maher-shalal-hash-baz?

2. Who was married to Elimelech and had sons
   named Mahlon and Chilion?

3. What same man did Michal, Abigail, and
   Ahinoam marry?

4. What were the complaints against Samuel's
   sons?

5. Who was King David's great-great-
   grandmother?

. . . .
Total possible points: 2,000
Your score: _____

1. Who were the four mothers of Jacob's twelve sons and one daughter?

2. Match the mothers from question 1 for Jacob's children: Reuben, Simeon, Levi, Judah, Dan, Naphtali, Gad, Asher, Issachar, Zebulon, Dinah, Joseph, and Benjamin.

3. How many siblings did Abram have, and what were their names?

4. What judge of Israel had seventy sons?

5. Who offered to sacrifice his daughter to God?

· · · · · · · · · · ·
Total possible points: 2,500
Your score: _____

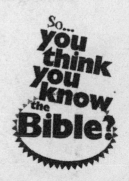

Quiz 2

• • • • • • • • • • • •

Relatives, Part 1

Total points for this quiz: 7,500
Your score for this quiz: _____

Running total, Quizzes 1–2: _____

Answers on page 224.

Quiz 3

Parables

People love mysteries—and Jesus' parables often sound rather enigmatic. Complete this quiz to unlock some of the Bible's parables.

• • • • • • • • •

1. What question was Jesus answering when He told the parable of the good Samaritan?

2. Whom did the five foolish virgins ask for oil for their lamps?

3. What did the parable of the vineyard owner teach about Jesus?

4. What parable taught that God will avenge His elect?

5. What parable did Jesus give following the parables of the lost sheep and the lost coin?

So...
you think you know the Bible?

• • • • • • • • • •
Total possible points: 500
Your score: _____

200 points each

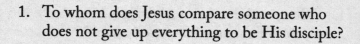

1. To whom does Jesus compare someone who does not give up everything to be His disciple?

2. Which parable includes "God be merciful to me a sinner"?

3. What did the merchant do when he found the pearl of great price?

4. What parable illustrates how God feels about those who don't forgive others?

5. How does the parable of the talents differ numerically from the parable of the pennies (denarii)?

. . . .
Total possible points: 1,000
Your score: _____

25

1. What prophet told an adulterous king the parable of a man with one ewe lamb?

2. What did Isaiah's parable of the vineyard say about Israel?

3. What parable included the concept of "eat, drink, and be merry"?

4. Under what two places did Jesus say that a lamp should not be put?

5. How many soils are described in the parable of the sower?

• • • • • • • • • •
Total possible points: 1,500
Your score: _____

1. What three hazards befell the seeds in Jesus' parable of the sower?

2. What parable illustrates the principle that no man can serve two masters?

3. Where was the man who was robbed going in the parable of the good Samaritan, and from where had he come?

4. What parable teaches that being rich doesn't automatically get you into heaven?

5. What parable ends with "wailing and gnashing of teeth"?

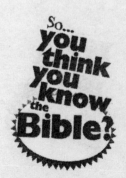

• • • • • • • • • • •

Total possible points: 2,000
Your score: _____

• • • • • • • • • •

1. Why didn't Jesus speak to His disciples in parables?

2. In Jesus' illustration of how God wants to give us good things, what did the Lord say a father would *not* give his son if he asked for bread?

3. To what did Jesus compare the mustard seed?

4. In what parable did Jesus tell the chief priests and elders that publicans and harlots would enter the kingdom of God before they did?

5. What parable ends with "So the last shall be first and the first last"?

• • • • • • • • • •

Total possible points: 2,500
Your score: _____

Quiz 3

• • • • • • • • • • •

Parables

Total points for this quiz: 7,500
Your score for this quiz: _____

Running total, Quizzes 1–3: _____

Answers on page 225.

Quiz 4

Places of Worship

The ancient Jewish tabernacle and the temple were filled with items of special significance to God. What do you know about those first places of worship?

1. What sacrifice were Mary and Joseph to make when they brought Jesus to the temple to present Him to the Lord?

2. How many loaves of the Bread of the Presence, or shewbread, were to be on the table in the tabernacle Sabbath after Sabbath?

3. How many pieces of gold were used to make the candlestick?

4. Who alone could enter the Holy of Holies and on what occasion?

5. Why wasn't David allowed to build the temple?

• • • • • • • • • • •
Total possible points: 500
Your score: _____

• • • • • • • • • • •

1. How long did it take Solomon to build the temple?

2. Why is there no temple in the New Jerusalem?

3. How often did the high priest burn incense on the golden altar?

4. Who was famous for making a detailed organization of temple personnel?

5. Who supplied the materials to build the tabernacle?

So...
you
think
you
know
the
Bible?

• • • • • • • • • • •

Total possible points: 1,000

Your score: _____

• • • • • • • • • • •

1. What were the holders on the lampstand in the tabernacle designed to look like?

2. What material was used to make the altar of incense in the tabernacle?

3. What separated the Holy Place from the Most Holy Place?

4. What material was to be used to make the tent pegs of the tabernacle?

5. What son of Shealtiel is credited with helping to rebuild the temple after the Babylonian captivity?

• • • • • • • • • • •

Total possible points: 1,500
Your score: _____

• • • • • • • • • • • •

1. Who destroyed Solomon's temple?

2. By what act could someone claim sanctuary in the temple?

3. When the Israelites moved into the Promised Land, what city became the permanent home of the tabernacle?

4. On what site did Solomon build the temple?

5. What two types of materials were used to make the curtains in the tabernacle?

So...
you think you know the Bible?

• • • • • • • • • • •

Total possible points: 2,000
Your score: _____

• • • • • • • • • • •

1. Where will the ark of the covenant ultimately be found?

2. On what article of the high priest's clothing were the Urim and Thummim placed?

3. How did God show His presence at the dedication of Solomon's temple?

4. How many days did the people celebrate following the completion of Solomon's temple?

5. What writer of Psalms was a supervisor of the music at Solomon's temple?

• • • • • • • • • • •

Total possible points: 2,500
Your score: _____

Quiz 4

• • • • • • • • • • •

Places of Worship

Total points for this quiz: 7,500
Your score for this quiz: _____

Running total, Quizzes 1–4: _____

Answers on page 226.

Quiz 5

Meanings of Words, Part 1

Most meanings of Bible names or words never actually appeared in the Bible—but there are some exceptions. See how well you can do, with or without a little help from a Bible dictionary.

• • • • • • • • • • •

1. What name for Jesus, meaning "Anointed One," did Daniel use when writing about the end times?

2. What name for Jesus, meaning "Anointed One," did the angel of the Lord use when speaking to the shepherds?

3. What patriarch, whose name means "laughter," was born to a woman who laughed when she learned she would be a mother?

4. What name for Jesus, meaning "God with us," was first used by Isaiah?

5. What did the name *Barnabas* mean?

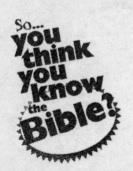

So...
you
think
you
know
the
Bible?

• • • • • • • • • •
Total possible points: 500
Your score: _____

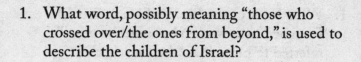

1. What word, possibly meaning "those who crossed over/the ones from beyond," is used to describe the children of Israel?

2. What word, meaning "our Lord will come," completes Paul's sentence: "Let him be Anathema _____"?

3. What word, which has been translated "astrologer," does Matthew use to describe certain visitors to Herod?

4. What name for Himself does God say He used when appearing to Abraham, Isaac, and Jacob?

5. What name for God has been translated "Father"?

• • • • • • • • • • •

Total possible points: 1,000
Your score: _____

1. What book of the Bible, which means "the Preacher," was written by someone who referred to himself as "the Preacher"?

2. What town, which means "house of bread," was near the site where Rachel was buried?

3. What does Ebenezer mean?

4. What word, which means "one separated," describes Samson?

5. What was the name of the valley from which came the word *Gehenna*, or "hell," where children were sacrificed by fire to pagan gods?

So...
you
think
you
know
the
Bible?

• • • • • • • • • •
Total possible points: 1,500
Your score: _____

• • • • • • • • • • • •

1. What name of God, which is *El-Elyon* in Hebrew, was used to describe the God whom the high priest Melchizedek served?

2. What Old Testament prophet, whose name means "God is my judge," was also known as Belteshazzar?

3. What woman, whose name means "princess," was described by God as a mother of nations?

4. What name, which means "bitter," did Naomi request that she be called?

5. What religious and political entity, whose name means "sitting together," tried to find false evidence against Jesus?

• • • • • • • • • •

Total possible points: 2,000
Your score: _____

So...
you
think
you
know
the
Bible?

• • • • • • • • • • • •

1. Whose name, which means "hasten the booty, hasten the spoils," was Isaiah directed to write with a man's pen in a great roll?

2. Who was called Ben-oni by his mother, a name that means "son of my sorrow"?

3. What Old Testament prophet, whose name means "my messenger," referred in his first chapter to Jacob and Esau?

4. What was the meaning of the handwriting on the wall: Mene, Mene, Tekel, Upharsin?

5. At what place, whose name means "oil press," did three disciples fall asleep?

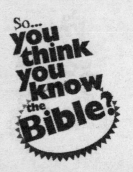
So...
you think you know the Bible?

• • • • • • • • • • •
Total possible points: 2,500
Your score: _____

Quiz 5

· · · · · · · · · · · ·

Meanings of Words, Part 1

Total points for this quiz: 7,500
Your score for this quiz: _____

Running total, Quizzes 1–5: _____

Answers on page 227.

Quiz 6

The Twelve Tribes

Imagine having *twelve* sons—that was the case for the patriarch Jacob, whose boys headed the twelve tribes of Israel. What do you remember about those tribes?

• • • • • • • • • • • •

1. From what tribe did Jesus descend?

2. What tribe had a book of the Bible named for them?

3. What tribe was Moses from?

4. What disciple of Jesus had the same name as one of the tribes?

5. What two tribes gathered, planning to make war against Israel to regain the kingdom for Rehoboam?

• • • • • • • • • • •

Total possible points: 500
Your score: _____

So...
you
think
you
know
the
Bible?

• • • • • • • • • • •

1. Who received the allotment for the tribe of Joseph?

2. What tribe must John the Baptist have come from?

3. In the city described in Revelation 21, are the twelve gates or the twelve foundations named for the tribes?

4. What word, which was difficult to pronounce, was used to trap the Ephraimites?

5. What king caused Israel to split into ten tribes and two tribes?

• • • • • • • • • • •

Total possible points: 1,000
Your score: _____

46

• • • • • • • • • • • •

1. What was the first tribe to set foot in the Promised Land?

2. Which of the tribes established its own idolatrous cult?

3. When the Israelites camped in the wilderness, on what side of the tabernacle did the tribes of Judah, Zebulun, and Issachar camp together?

4. What was the function of the Levites who were not priests?

5. In Matthew 10:5–6, how did Jesus refer to the twelve tribes of Israel?

• • • • • • • • • • •

Total possible points: 1,500
Your score: _____

So...
you think you know the Bible?

• • • • • • • • • • • •

1. What New Testament book is specifically addressed to the twelve tribes?

2. Against which tribe did the children of Israel wage war for evil done to the concubine of a Levite?

3. For what was the tribe of Benjamin famous?

4. Which tribe was often identified as a "half tribe"?

5. After the tribes were split into the kingdoms of Israel and Judah, by what tribal name was the kingdom of Israel referred?

So...
you
think
you
know
the
Bible?

• • • • • • • • • • •
Total possible points: 2,000
Your score: _____

1. What tribe, which could not occupy its allotted place in the Promised Land, took over somewhere else?

2. How many from the tribes of Israel are "sealed" in the book of Revelation?

3. Which tribe, according to Jacob's blessing, was "a hind let loose"?

4. What tribes settled east of the Jordan River?

5. What tribe settled north and northwest of the Sea of Galilee?

· · · · · · · · · · · ·

Total possible points: 2,500
Your score: _____

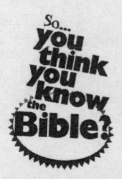

The Twelve Tribes

Total points for this quiz: 7,500
Your score for this quiz: _____

Running total, Quizzes 1–6: _____

Answers on page 228.

Quiz 7

The Holy Spirit

The Holy Spirit works in mysterious ways. Here is a quiz to help you discover some of those ways.

• • • • • • • • • •

1. In Genesis 1:2, what was the Spirit of the Lord doing?

2. Who tried to buy the gifts of the Holy Spirit?

3. What name did Jesus use for the Holy Spirit?

4. After Pentecost, how did the apostles impart the Holy Spirit?

5. Through the laying on of whose hands did Timothy receive the Holy Spirit?

So...
you
think
you
know
the
Bible?

• • • • • • • • • • •
Total possible points: 500
Your score: _____

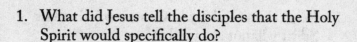
1. What did Jesus tell the disciples that the Holy Spirit would specifically do?

2. On what New Testament occasion were the Holy Spirit, God the Father, and Jesus all present at the same time?

3. How did the Holy Spirit empower Moses' seventy elders?

4. What does 1 Corinthians 2:12 say that the Holy Spirit is not the spirit of?

5. The Holy Spirit bears witness with us that we are what to God?

Total possible points: 1,000
Your score: _____

• • • • • • • • • • •

1. What does God say in Genesis 6:3 that His Spirit will not always do?

2. What are five symbols of the Holy Spirit?

3. According to the prophet Joel, what would the Holy Spirit enable young men and young women to do?

4. Using Paul's belt (or "girdle"), what message from the Holy Spirit did Agabus give Paul?

5. According to Paul, what will we not fulfill if we walk in the Spirit?

So...
you
think
you
know
the
Bible?

• • • • • • • • • • •
Total possible points: 1,500
Your score: _____

1. What does Romans 8:26 say that the Holy
    Spirit does for us?

2. According to Acts 8:39, what did the Holy
    Spirit do with Philip?

3. What three things did Paul tell Timothy that
    God has given us, as opposed to a spirit of
    fear?

4. How do those who do not have God's Spirit
    consider the things of God?

5. What did Jesus do to the disciples, after His
    resurrection, before He gave them His Spirit?

• • • • • • • • • • •

Total possible points: 2,000
Your score: _____

1. According to Paul, in whom have we been marked with a seal?

2. According to Paul, for what four things are the Holy Spirit–inspired scriptures profitable?

3. What should we not do to the Holy Spirit?

4. According to Paul, how should we endeavor to keep the unity of the Spirit?

5. According to John, what does the Holy Spirit help us do?

So...
you
think
you
know
the
Bible?

• • • • • • • • • • •
Total possible points: 2,500
Your score: _____

Quiz 7

• • • • • • • • • •

The Holy Spirit

Total points for this quiz: 7,500
Your score for this quiz: _____

Running total, Quizzes 1–7: _____

Answers on page 229.

Quiz 8

Angels

Forget those old paintings—angels aren't described as chubby kids with wings. Do you know what the Bible actually says about them?

100 points each

• • • • • • • • • • •

1. Who is described by Paul as being "transformed into an angel of light"?

2. What was Michael's title?

3. How many times did the angel of the Lord speak to Abraham during the attempted sacrifice of Isaac?

4. What does Psalm 78:25 refer to as angels' food?

5. What animal saw the angel of the Lord?

• • • • • • • • • • •

Total possible points: 500
Your score: _____

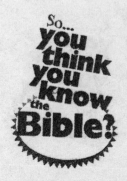

1. Who saw Satan fall as lightning from heaven?

2. What did the angels who visited Sodom do with Lot?

3. Besides Jacob, to whom did the angel of the Lord appear in a dream?

4. What devout Gentile received a visit from the angel of the Lord?

5. In addition to Peter, whom did an angel let out of jail?

• • • • • • • • • • •
Total possible points: 1,000
Your score: _____

• • • • • • • • • • • • •

1. According to Daniel 12:1, what was one of Michael's jobs?

2. Around whom does the angel of the Lord encamp?

3. Who was struck by an angel and eaten by worms?

4. Whom does Paul say God made a spectacle to the angels, the world, and men?

5. Who will judge the angels?

• • • • • • • • • • •

Total possible points: 1,500
Your score: _____

• • • • • • • • • • • •

1. Who was the cherub appointed to oversee the Garden of Eden?

2. In which two books do we learn that the angel Michael has face-to-face confrontations with Satan?

3. Who talked about an angel who had redeemed him from evil?

4. Who convinced a prophet to sin by claiming he had a message from the angel of the Lord?

5. In Isaiah 63:9, whom does Isaiah say God used to save His people?

• • • • • • • • • • • •

Total possible points: 2,000
Your score: _____

• • • • • • • • • •

1. To which three people did Gabriel appear?

2. What job was given to cherubim after the expulsion of Adam and Eve from Eden?

3. What was the purpose for the three pairs of wings on the seraphim?

4. What judge of Israel was afraid he was going to die because he saw the angel of the Lord?

5. Who was described as being as "good in my sight as an angel of God"?

• • • • • • • • • • •

Total possible points: 2,500
Your score: _____

Quiz 8

• • • • • • • • • • •

Angels

Total points for this quiz: 7,500
Your score for this quiz: _____

Running total, Quizzes 1–8: _____

Answers on page 230.

Quiz 9

Priests

High priests did the work of the Lord—
or at least they were supposed to. What
do you know about the priests themselves,
the tools of their trade, and their recorded
actions?

1. What was the short outer garment priests wore over their robes?

2. What high priest anointed Solomon as king?

3. What was the three-step process of appointing a high priest?

4. What priest also served as a scribe, documenting the return of the Babylonian captives to Jerusalem?

5. What priest was also a king?

So...
you
think
you
know
the
Bible?

• • • • • • • • • • •
Total possible points: 500
Your score: _____

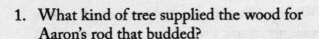

1. What kind of tree supplied the wood for Aaron's rod that budded?

2. What annual occasion witnessed the priest using the scapegoat?

3. What noisemakers hung off the hem of the priest's garment?

4. Which New Testament writer says we are a holy priesthood, a royal priesthood?

5. What king made priests from every class of people, an act that destroyed his house?

Total possible points: 1,000
Your score: _____

• • • • • • • • • • •

1. What priest kept Joash safe when all Joash's siblings were killed?

2. What priest had sons named Hophni and Phinehas?

3. What was engraved on the front of the high priest's turban?

4. Who killed all of Ahab's household, including his priests?

5. What high priest in King Josiah's reign discovered the book of the law while repairing the temple?

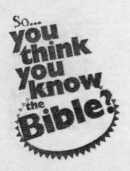

So...
you think you know the Bible?

• • • • • • • • • •
Total possible points: 1,500
Your score: _____

1. What high priest said it was expedient that one man should die for the people?

2. Whose wife was the daughter of an Egyptian priest?

3. How many cities were allotted to the priests in the Promised Land?

4. What high priest did Paul call a whitewashed wall?

5. What king was condemned for acting as a priest?

• • • • • • • • • •

Total possible points: 2,000
Your score: _____

So...
you
think
you
know
the
Bible?

1. To what priestly division did Zechariah belong?

2. What priest allowed David to eat the shewbread?

3. What were the seven sons of the priest Sceva trying to do?

4. What priest during the reign of King Ahaz built an altar based on the design of an altar in Damascus?

5. What part of Jerusalem during Nehemiah's time did the high priest Eliashib build?

• • • • • • • • • •

Total possible points: 2,500
Your score: _____

Quiz 9

• • • • • • • • • •

Priests

Total points for this quiz: 7,500
Your score for this quiz: _____

Running total, Quizzes 1–9: _____

Answers on page 231.

Quiz 10

Prophecies

Some prophecies are well-known, but others are not so obvious. What do you know about these?

1. When God told Abram to leave Ur, what did He promise him?

2. What minor prophet predicted that the Messiah would be betrayed for thirty pieces of silver?

3. What minor prophet's book contains the prophecy that the Messiah would be born in Bethlehem?

4. What was the fulfillment of the prophecy "Out of Egypt have I called my son"?

5. Who wrote the prophecy "I am poured out like water, and all my bones are out of joint"?

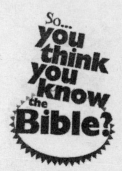

• • • • • • • • • • •

Total possible points: 500
Your score: _____

1. What did the curse pronounced on Ham say would happen to his descendants?

2. When Jesus prophesied that the temple would be destroyed, what description did He use?

3. What famous relative of Jesus did Isaiah and Malachi both foretell?

4. What did the four beasts represent in Daniel's vision?

5. When Jesus prophesied about His death, which minor prophet did He say was a sign?

So...
you
think
you
know
the
Bible?

• • • • • • • • • •
Total possible points: 1,000
Your score: _____

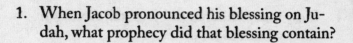

1. When Jacob pronounced his blessing on Judah, what prophecy did that blessing contain?

2. What was the meaning of Ezekiel's vision of dry bones that shook and then formed a body?

3. What ruler did Jeremiah prophesy would allow the Israelites to return from Babylon?

4. When did Jesus say that the disciples would be witnesses to Him?

5. Where in the Old Testament is the prophecy about Jesus being bruised for our iniquities?

Total possible points: 1,500
Your score: _____

• • • • • • • • • • •

1. How many children did God tell Abraham Ishmael would have?

2. What minor prophet prophesied about the outpouring of God's Spirit at Pentecost?

3. In Jacob's dream of the ladder stretching to heaven, to what were Jacob's descendants compared?

4. To what time in the Old Testament did Jesus compare the time when the Son of Man will return?

5. What vision did God send Paul to call him to preach to the Gentiles?

So...
you
think
you
know
the
Bible?

• • • • • • • • • • •

Total possible points: 2,000
Your score: _____

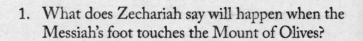

1. What does Zechariah say will happen when the Messiah's foot touches the Mount of Olives?

2. What did Joseph dream the sun, the moon, and eleven stars did?

3. To whom was David referring when he wrote, "Mine own familiar friend, in whom I trusted, which did eat of my bread, has lifted up his heel against me"?

4. What person and group of people did Jesus tell the Pharisees would rise up in judgment of them?

5. What event that Agabus prophesied happened in the days of Claudius Caesar?

Total possible points: 2,500
Your score: _____

So...
you
think
you
know
the
Bible?

Quiz 10

• • • • • • • • • •

Prophecies

Total points for this quiz: 7,500
Your score for this quiz: _____

Running total, Quizzes 1–10: _____

Answers on page 232.

Quiz 11

Numbers

You don't have to be a math whiz to answer these questions. You just have to know your Bible pretty well.

1. How many chapters does the book of Habakkuk have?

2. How many days did Noah wait, after he had sent out the raven and the dove, before he sent out the dove again?

3. How old were Abraham and Sarah when Isaac was born?

4. How many children did Job have?

5. How many windows and doors did Noah's ark have?

● ● ● ● ● ● ● ● ● ●
Total possible points: 500
Your score: _____

200 points each

• • • • • • • • • • • •

1. What famous king had seven hundred wives?

2. How old was Abraham when Ishmael was born?

3. How high was the gallows Haman built?

4. How long was Moses on Mount Sinai the second time?

5. How many cubits did Jesus say we can add to our stature?

• • • • • • • • • • • •
Total possible points: 1,000
Your score: _____

• • • • • • • • • • •

1. Approximately how many souls were added to the church on Pentecost?

2. How many were in Jacob's group when he moved to Egypt?

3. How many sons did Naomi and Elimelech have?

4. How many days did Daniel eat "pulse and water"?

5. How old was Jesus when he left Mary and Joseph to be in the temple?

• • • • • • • • • •

Total possible points: 1,500
Your score: _____

400 points each

• • • • • • • • • • •

1. How many judges were there in Israel?

2. How many people did God tell Elijah there were who had never bowed the knee to Baal?

3. How old was Methuselah when he died?

4. How many were in a group appointed by Jesus to arrive in cities before He did?

5. How many rows of stones were set in the breastplate that Aaron wore?

• • • • • • • • • • •

Total possible points: 2,000
Your score: _____

• • • • • • • • • • • •

1. What five books of the Bible have only one chapter?

2. How long had the king and his satraps been feasting at the start of the book of Esther?

3. How old was Noah when the flood came?

4. How long did the Philistines keep the ark of the covenant, after they captured it, before returning it to Israel?

5. How long was the ark of the covenant kept in Kirjath-jearim?

So...
you
think
you
know
the
Bible?

• • • • • • • • • • •
Total possible points: 2,500
Your score: _____

Quiz 11

• • • • • • • • • •

Numbers

Total points for this quiz: 7,500
Your score for this quiz: _____

Running total, Quizzes 1–11: _____

Answers on page 233.

Quiz 12

Who's Who in
the New Testament

Two thousand years ago, just like today, some people followed Jesus' example, and others didn't. What do you know about these people from the New Testament?

1. Who held discarded coats while Stephen was being stoned?

2. What were the Bereans famous for?

3. Who was the thirteenth apostle?

4. What name did the following people have in common: son of Alphaeus, brother of the apostle Judas (not Iscariot), brother of Jesus?

5. Which two apostles raised people from the dead?

• • • • • • • • • • •

Total possible points: 500
Your score: _____

1. Who was Philemon's runaway slave?

2. Which disciple brought the boy with the two loaves and five fishes to Jesus?

3. Who were Paul's three primary coworkers on his missionary journeys?

4. In addition to Paul, what other preacher did Priscilla and Aquila work with, even teaching him the gospel?

5. Who was commanded to go lay hands on Saul (Paul) so that he would regain his sight?

• • • • • • • • • •
Total possible points: 1,000
Your score: _____

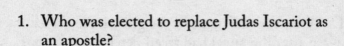

1. Who was elected to replace Judas Iscariot as an apostle?

2. Whom did Paul circumcise and whom did he refuse to have circumcised?

3. What were Barabbas's crimes?

4. Who addressed the Sanhedrin with a face like an angel?

5. How many descriptions are given of Judas Iscariot's death?

Total possible points: 1,500
Your score: _____

1. What was the name of the girl who let Peter in after the angel had freed Peter from prison?

2. What apostle mentions Paul by name in his Bible book?

3. In addition to betraying Jesus, what other crime did Judas Iscariot commit?

4. What was the name of the evil spirit that possessed the man who lived in the tombs?

5. Who had their mother ask Jesus for seats of honor for them in His kingdom?

• • • • • • • • • • •
Total possible points: 2,000
Your score: _____

1. Name five Simons mentioned in the New Testament.

2. Who were the only people Paul said he baptized?

3. What silversmith made shrines of the goddess Diana in Ephesus?

4. Why were the seven chosen in Acts 6?

5. Who were the two women Paul urged to get along together in Philippians 4:2?

· · · · · · · · ·

Total possible points: 2,500
Your score: _____

Quiz 12

• • • • • • • • • • •

Who's Who in
the New Testament

Total points for this quiz: 7,500
Your score for this quiz: _____

Running total, Quizzes 1–12: _____

Answers on page 234.

Quiz 13

Occupations

Bible characters held some interesting jobs. Would you want any of these?

1. What job was Moses doing when God spoke to him from the burning bush?

2. With whom were James and John partners?

3. What did Priscilla and Aquila do when they weren't teaching the gospel?

4. Who did Delilah work for?

5. What was the occupation of the Ethiopian eunuch in Acts 8?

• • • • • • • • • • •

Total possible points: 500
Your score: _____

• • • • • • • • • • • •

1. For which two of Pharaoh's servants did Joseph interpret dreams?

2. What was Pontius Pilate's job?

3. Who were two tax collectors associated with Jesus?

4. Who is the only witch mentioned in the Bible?

5. Before which two governors, whose names both begin with *F*, did Paul appear?

• • • • • • • • • • •

Total possible points: 1,000
Your score: _____

So...
**you
think
you
know
the
Bible?**

• • • • • • • • • • •

1. Who was King Artaxerxes' cupbearer?

2. What position did Joseph hold in Egypt?

3. Who told Naaman to go see the prophet and be healed?

4. What job did Abel, Rachel, and Zipporah have in common?

5. What metals did Tubalcain work with?

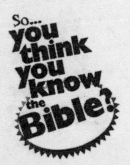

• • • • • • • • • • •
Total possible points: 1,500
Your score: _____

• • • • • • • • • • • •

1. What did Amos do before he was a prophet?

2. What was Luke's occupation?

3. What was Potiphar's job?

4. What occupation did Paul say the law held in regard to us?

5. What is the occupation of the man other than the Pharisee in the parable of the two men who go to the temple to pray?

• • • • • • • • • • •

Total possible points: 2,000
Your score: _____

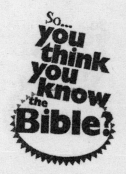

• • • • • • • • • • • •

1. Who was appointed governor of Judah by Nebuchadnezzar?

2. What did Nebuchadnezzar appoint Shadrach, Meshach, and Abednego to do?

3. What did Zimri do before he became king of Israel?

4. Who was the priest of Midian?

5. What did Huldah and Anna have in common?

So...
you think you know the Bible?

• • • • • • • • • •
Total possible points: 2,500
Your score: _____

Quiz 13

. . . .
Occupations

Total points for this quiz: 7,500
Your score for this quiz: _____

Running total, Quizzes 1–13: _____

Answers on page 235.

Quiz 14

God

Awesome, majestic, all-powerful, loving—
the list goes on and on. How much more
do you know about God?

• • • • • • • • • • • •

1. What does Romans 1 say reveals the invisible attributes of God?

2. When Moses asked God whom he should say sent him, what name did God tell him to use?

3. Who served as Israel's advocate and talked God out of killing the children of Israel?

4. How many days did God take to create the world?

5. How did Jesus say we are to worship God?

• • • • • • • • • • •

Total possible points: 500
Your score: _____

1. Who was known as the man after God's own heart?

2. Who was known as the friend of God?

3. What did God tell Moses would keep the diseases of the Egyptians from afflicting the Israelites?

4. Whom did God tell in a dream not to talk to Herod?

5. What, according to the psalmist, declares the glory of God?

· · · · · · · · · · · ·

Total possible points: 1,000
Your score: _____

• • • • • • • • • • • •

1. On what occasion did God "repent," or regret something He had done?

2. When will God wipe away all tears and eliminate death?

3. What reason does David give in Psalm 35 to persuade God to smite his enemies?

4. In what Old Testament book can you read that Satan goes before God's face?

5. Who called God "the one who sees"?

• • • • • • • • • • • •

Total possible points: 1,500
Your score: _____

• • • • • • • • • • • •

1. When Jesus was on earth, on what two occasions did God speak directly from heaven?

2. How long does the psalmist say that a thousand years are in God's sight?

3. What saying in Deuteronomy 6:4 did the Israelites use as a call to worship?

4. What does John 3:17 say that God did not send Jesus to do?

5. What was cursed by God because of Adam?

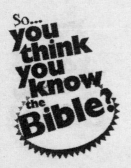

So...
you
think
you
know
the
Bible?

• • • • • • • • • •
Total possible points: 2,000
Your score: _____

500 points each

• • • • • • • • • • • •

1. Who was described as walking with God, and then God "took him"?

2. When Elijah was on Mount Horeb, what three things did God show him?

3. According to the writer of Proverbs, what seven things are an abomination to God?

4. What did God claim as sanctified unto Him, both of man and beast?

5. According to Zephaniah 3:17, how does God feel about His people?

• • • • • • • • • • •

Total possible points: 2,500
Your score: _____

Quiz 14

• • • • • • • • • • •

God

Total points for this quiz: 7,500
Your score for this quiz: _____

Running total, Quizzes 1–14: _____

Answers on page 236.

Quiz 15

By Any Other Name

Some familiar people and things also had less familiar alternative names. Test your knowledge of multiple monikers!

1. Who were the "sons of thunder"?

2. By what other name is Passover known?

3. Who was referred to as a skilled player on the harp?

4. Whose description included the fact that he ate locusts and honey?

5. In Jesus' genealogy in Matthew 1, who is referred to as the "wife of Uriah"?

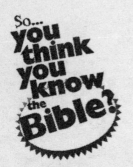

• • • • • • • • • • •

Total possible points: 500
Your score: _____

1. What did Rachel first name Benjamin?

2. What was Esther's Hebrew name?

3. What was the result of Jacob's wrestling with the angel?

4. What disciple was known also as Levi?

5. Who was the "ambassador in bonds"?

• • • • • • • • • • •

Total possible points: 1,000
Your score: _____

• • • • • • • • • • • •

1. Who was described as having found grace in the eyes of the Lord?

2. By what other names do we know Hananiah, Mishael, and Azariah?

3. What was the potter's field also known as?

4. What two descriptions of Satan appear in Revelation 12:9?

5. What ruler in Egypt was called Zaphnath-paaneah?

So...
you think you know the Bible?

• • • • • • • • • • • •
Total possible points: 1,500
Your score: _____

• • • • • • • • • • •

1. What was Daniel's Babylonian name?

2. To what did Naomi want to change her name?

3. Who is described in Hebrews as the "author and finisher of our faith"?

4. When Solomon built the temple, what did he name Jachin and Boaz?

5. What judge's other name was Jerubbaal?

• • • • • • • • • •

Total possible points: 2,000
Your score: _____

• • • • • • • • • • •

1. Who was known as a mighty hunter before God?

2. What early Bible figure was described as the father of those who dwell in tents?

3. By what description do we know the following group of men: Shammua, Shaphat, Igal, Palti, Gaddiel, Gaddi, Ammiel, Sethur, Nahbi, Geuel?

4. What more familiar name now applies to the ancient city of Jebus?

5. What was Euroclydon?

• • • • • • • • • • •

Total possible points: 2,500

Your score: _____

Quiz 15

. . . .

By Any Other Name

Total points for this quiz: 7,500
Your score for this quiz: _____

Running total, Quizzes 1–15: _____

Answers on page 237.

Quiz 16

Prophets

Whether famous or unknown, God's prophets had intriguing and eventful lives. What do you know about these seers?

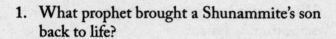

1. What prophet brought a Shunammite's son back to life?

2. How many kings did Isaiah serve as a prophet?

3. When Daniel first arrived in Babylon, what did he immediately refuse to do?

4. Who was the first prophet?

5. What prophet had a live coal put on his mouth?

Total possible points: 500
Your score: _____

• • • • • • • • • •

1. What two minor prophets prophesied at the same time as Isaiah?

2. What was the name of Jeremiah's scribe?

3. What prophet told a king that he would be as an ox and eat grass in the field?

4. What prophet said, "Can two walk together, except they be agreed?"

5. Who was the prophet who literally ate the Word of the Lord?

So...
you think you know the Bible?

• • • • • • • • • •

Total possible points: 1,000
Your score: _____

1. What king burned the scroll of Jeremiah's prophecies?

2. Who had four daughters who prophesied?

3. What Old Testament prophet describes a city similar to the one in Revelation 21?

4. What prophet's bones revived a dead man?

5. What prophet had two children whose names meant "not loved" and "not my people"?

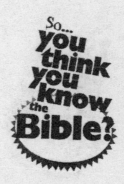

Total possible points: 1,500
Your score: _____

1. What king did the prophet Nathan help anoint?

2. What happened to the prophet who ate and drank when God told him not to?

3. Who did Samuel say would prophesy and be "turned into another man"?

4. What prophet got so angry at God that he told God to just go ahead and kill him?

5. When the disciples asked Jesus to tell them the signs of His coming and the end of the age, what prophet did Jesus quote?

So...
you
think
you
know
the
Bible?

• • • • • • • • • • •
Total possible points: 2,000
Your score: _____

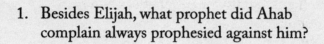
1. Besides Elijah, what prophet did Ahab complain always prophesied against him?

2. For how long was Ezekiel commanded to lie on his left side?

3. What prophet was commanded to marry an unfaithful wife?

4. Of what country did Obadiah prophesy?

5. What false prophet prophesied against Jeremiah and died?

Total possible points: 2,500
Your score: _____

Quiz 16

• • • • • • • • • • •

Prophets

Total points for this quiz: 7,500
Your score for this quiz: _____

Running total, Quizzes 1–16: _____

Answers on page 238.

Quiz 17

Royalty,
Part 1

The Bible is full of good and bad kings.
So is this quiz.

• • • • • • • • • • •

1. What wicked king and queen killed Naboth so they could steal his vineyard?

2. What king drove his chariot furiously?

3. Who was queen of Persia before Esther?

4. Who was king of Salem?

5. Who does the Bible say did evil in the sight of the Lord more than all who were before him?

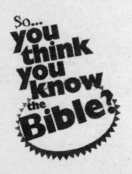

So...
you
think
you
know
the
Bible?

• • • • • • • • • • •
Total possible points: 500
Your score: _____

1. What horrible thing did Athaliah do?

2. What king sent cedars to both David and Solomon?

3. What Babylonian king commandeered Judah into captivity?

4. What name applies to a line of wicked kings from the time of Jesus through the apostle Paul?

5. What king solicited the services of the witch of Endor?

• • • • • • • • • • •
Total possible points: 1,000
Your score: _____

1. Why did God give Solomon riches, wealth, and honor?

2. What royal heir got hanged by his hair in a tree?

3. For what king of Moab did Balaam work?

4. Whose feelings were hurt because Israel wanted a king?

5. What king threw Daniel into the lions' den?

• • • • • • • • • • •

Total possible points: 1,500
Your score: _____

• • • • • • • • • • • •

1. Who was the last king of Israel?

2. Who was the last king of Judah?

3. What king took Israel into captivity to Assyria?

4. Who tried to take over as king when David died?

5. Besides king of Judea, what was Herod's other title?

• • • • • • • • • • •

Total possible points: 2,000
Your score: _____

125

1. What ruler followed Joash as king of Israel?

2. What king did Saul refuse to kill in direct disobedience to God's command?

3. What king got a withered hand because he tried to have a prophet arrested?

4. How did Jezebel die?

5. Over what people was Balak king?

Total possible points: 2,500
Your score: _____

126

Quiz 17

• • • • • • • • • • • •

Royalty,
Part 1

Total points for this quiz: 7,500
Your score for this quiz: _____

Running total, Quizzes 1–17: _____

Answers on page 239.

Quiz 18

Jesus

One day, every knee will bow to Jesus Christ. How much do you know about Him?

100 points each

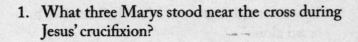

1. What three Marys stood near the cross during Jesus' crucifixion?

2. What two groups motivated Jesus to say, "They be blind leaders of the blind"?

3. Who was promised that he would not die until he saw the Messiah come?

4. Who was the first person to see Jesus after His resurrection?

5. When someone called Jesus "good Master," what did Jesus reply?

Total possible points: 500
Your score: _____

So... you think you know the Bible?

• • • • • • • • • • • •

1. To whom did Jesus say, "Man shall not live by bread alone"?

2. Who was Jesus' first disciple?

3. Who was Caesar when Jesus was born?

4. Why was Jesus in Jerusalem when he got separated from His parents?

5. How long did Jesus' parents search before they found Him?

So...
**you
think
you
know
the
Bible?**

• • • • • • • • • • •

Total possible points: 1,000
Your score: _____

• • • • • • • • • • •

1. Who are the four women mentioned in Jesus' genealogy in Matthew 1?

2. From what mountain did Jesus talk about the end times?

3. What miracle did Jesus perform in a synagogue on the Sabbath?

4. Who paid Judas Iscariot to betray Jesus?

5. What did the people shout when Jesus rode into Jerusalem on Palm Sunday?

• • • • • • • • • • •

Total possible points: 1,500
Your score: _____

1. When the chief priests and elders demanded to know by what authority Jesus taught, what question did Jesus use to confound them?

2. According to Paul, how was Jesus in the wilderness with Moses and the children of Israel?

3. How many days had Lazarus lain in the tomb before Jesus arrived at the site?

4. Who buried Jesus?

5. What were Jesus' last words on the cross?

• • • • • • • • • • •

Total possible points: 2,000
Your score: _____

· · · · · · · · · · ·

1. What are five "I am" descriptions that Jesus used to describe Himself?

2. How did Pilate's wife describe Jesus?

3. Who described Jesus as the "Lamb of God who takes away the sin of the world"?

4. When Jesus sent forth His twelve disciples the first time, what did He give them the power and authority to do?

5. Which of the following are not ancestors of Jesus? Jeconiah, Salmon, Zerubbabel, Jeroboam, Saul, Athaliah, Zedekiah, Daniel, Obed

· · · · · · · · · · ·

Total possible points: 2,500
Your score: _____

Quiz 18

• • • • • • • • • • •

Jesus

Total points for this quiz: 7,500
Your score for this quiz: _____

Running total, Quizzes 1–18: _____

Answers on page 240.

Quiz 19

Geography

There are almost as many places in the Bible as there are people. What do you know about these places?

. . . .

1. Upon what mountain did Elijah defeat the prophets of Baal?

2. What patriarch went out not knowing where he went?

3. When God told Jonah to go to Nineveh, to what city did Jonah try to flee?

4. What was Abram's point of origin?

5. From what location did Moses send the twelve spies into the Promised Land?

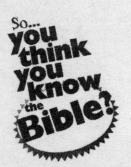

. . . .

Total possible points: 500
Your score: _____

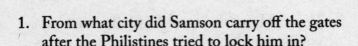
1. From what city did Samson carry off the gates after the Philistines tried to lock him in?

2. At what site did the Lord confound the language of the earth?

3. Where was Ezekiel when he began to prophesy?

4. Where was the Garden of Gethsemane located?

5. Where did Lazarus and his sisters live?

• • • • • • • • • • •
Total possible points: 1,000
Your score: _____

• • • • • • • • • • •

1. When Moses fled from Egypt, to what country did he go?

2. Out of what city was Paul lowered in a basket over the wall?

3. Where was the Pool of Bethesda, and what was special about it?

4. What are Pison, Gihon, Hiddekel, and Euphrates?

5. Where were the two disciples headed when Jesus walked with them after His resurrection?

• • • • • • • • • • •

Total possible points: 1,500
Your score: _____

1. Toward the end of his life, Jeremiah was taken captive to what country?

2. Where was Eve in the Garden of Eden when the serpent spoke to her?

3. Where was Adam when the serpent spoke to Eve?

4. What was the "great city," or capital, of Assyria?

5. From what mountain was Moses given a look into the Promised Land?

• • • • • • • • • • •

Total possible points: 2,000
Your score: _____

• • • • • • • • • • •

1. When Moses died, in what land did God bury him?

2. Where did Paul meet Aquila and Priscilla?

3. Of what significance was Mount Hor to Aaron?

4. To what city did Jesus lead His disciples just before His ascension?

5. What did Abraham name the place where God told him to sacrifice Isaac?

So...
you
think
you
know
the
Bible?

• • • • • • • • • • •

Total possible points: 2,500
Your score: _____

Quiz 19

• • • • • • • • • •

Geography

Total points for this quiz: 7,500
Your score for this quiz: _____

Running total, Quizzes 1–19: _____

Answers on page 241.

Meanings of Words, Part 2

What's in a name? The Bible proves there's plenty. Try your hand at these.

• • • • • • • • • • •

1. What king, whose name means "peaceable,"
   hosted the queen of Sheba?

2. What group of men, identified by a name
   that means "messenger," will have their names
   written on the walls of the New Jerusalem?

3. Which day of the week, which means
   "cessation from labor," was made for man?

4. What woman, whose name means "living,"
   was mother to Seth?

5. What does *Golgotha* mean?

• • • • • • • • • • •

Total possible points: 500
Your score: _____

1. What Old Testament book, which means "second law," depicts the death of Moses?

2. What woman, whose name means "friendship," was the great-grandmother of King David?

3. What region, whose name means "watch tower," was the homeland of the woman Jesus met at the well?

4. What man, whose name means "son of the father," was released by Pilate?

5. What city, whose name means "house of God," was the site of an altar built by Jacob?

• • • • • • • • • • •
Total possible points: 1,000
Your score: _____

1. What great star in the book of Revelation, whose name means "bitter," fell upon the third part of the rivers?

2. Who is the angel of the bottomless pit, whose name means "the destroyer," in the book of Revelation?

3. Who was the first of Job's three daughters of his second family, a name that means "dove"?

4. What is the name that means "wickedness," which is referred to in the Old Testament as being a father to children who worship other gods?

5. What patriarch, whose name means "supplanter," was the favorite of his mother?

• • • • • • • • • • •

Total possible points: 1,500
Your score: _____

So...
**you
think
you
know
the
Bible?**

1. What was *Corban*, in simplest terms?

2. What was the Persian word for "casting lots"?

3. What woman, whose name can mean "insolence" or "large," was known for her scarlet cord?

4. What false god, whose name means "master," was destroyed by Gideon?

5. What false goddess, called by some "the queen of heaven," was pursued by Solomon?

So...
you think you know the Bible?

• • • • • • • • • • • •
Total possible points: 2,000
Your score: _____

• • • • • • • • • • •

1. What empire, whose name means "gate of God," once sent a get-well gift to King Hezekiah?

2. What prophet, whose name means "Yahweh is my God," was known as the Tishbite?

3. What prophet, whose name means "God has granted salvation," once healed the waters with salt?

4. What official, whose name means "happy," trembled at Paul's preaching?

5. What place did the Lord name that means "Is the Lord among us or not?"

• • • • • • • • • • •

Total possible points: 2,500
Your score: _____

Quiz 20

• • • • • • • • • • •

Meanings of Words,
Part 2

Total points for this quiz: 7,500
Your score for this quiz: _____

Running total, Quizzes 1–20: _____

Answers on page 242.

Quiz 21

Hodgepodge

Every quiz needs a catchall category. Here are some questions that wouldn't fit anywhere else.

1. What is the incense on the altar in Revelation 8:4?

2. What was Jesus being questioned about when He said, "Render unto Caesar the things that are Caesar's"?

3. What word completes Jesus' saying, "Many are called, but few are _____"?

4. What word completes this saying in Isaiah, "Though [your sins] be red like crimson, they shall be as _____"?

5. On what day of Passover was leavened bread to be put out of the Israelites' houses?

So...
you
think
you
know
the
Bible?

• • • • • • • • • • •
Total possible points: 500
Your score: _____

• • • • • • • • • •

1. What musical instrument does the psalmist describe as loud and high sounding?

2. Who told Job to curse God and die?

3. What was created first, the seas or the stars?

4. What Old Testament feast was celebrated every month?

5. In addition to one body, one Spirit, one hope, one Lord, one faith, and one baptism, what else does Ephesians 4:6 say we have one of?

• • • • • • • • • • •

Total possible points: 1,000
Your score: _____

1. According to God, of what kind of wood was
    the ark to be made?

2. What herbs did Jesus say the Pharisees tithed?

3. Who was Ezekiel's father?

4. What Old Testament festival lasted seven
    days?

5. Where did Paul meet Lydia?

Total possible points: 1,500
Your score: _____

1. What punishment did God give humankind because their every thought was evil continually?

2. How often did the year of Jubilee occur?

3. By what symbolic gesture did the kinsman turn over his rights concerning Ruth to Boaz?

4. Why did Priscilla and Aquila live in Corinth?

5. Where did Paul find the altar inscribed "To the Unknown God"?

• • • • • • • • • • •

Total possible points: 2,000
Your score: _____

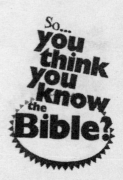

• • • • • • • • • • • •

1. What are the seven churches listed in Revelation 2–3?

2. Where did the valiant men bury Saul's bones?

3. When the Pharisees tried to trick Jesus in the matter of paying taxes, what type of coin did they show Him?

4. According to the writer of the book of Acts, how far was it from the Mount of Olives to Jerusalem?

5. What two groups of philosophers questioned Paul in Athens?

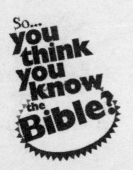

So...
you think you know the Bible?

• • • • • • • • • •

Total possible points: 2,500
Your score: _____

Quiz 21

. . . .

Hodgepodge

Total points for this quiz: 7,500
Your score for this quiz: _____

Running total, Quizzes 1–21: _____

Answers on page 243.

Quiz 22

Animal, Vegetable, Mineral

Remember the game of twenty questions? Well, here are twenty-five for you, but these can't be answered with a simple yes or no.

1. What two animals did David boast of killing?

2. How many of each clean animal did Noah take on the ark?

3. Besides manna, what did God provide in the wilderness for the children of Israel to eat?

4. How did John the Baptist address Jesus when he saw Him by the Jordan?

5. Which of Jesus' parables contained a feast with a fattened calf?

• • • • • • • • • • •

Total possible points: 500
Your score: _____

• • • • • • • • • •

1. When Noah got off the ark, what did he plant?

2. What type of tree did Zacchaeus climb in order to see Jesus?

3. What did the four living creatures around the throne resemble, respectively?

4. What was the sacrifice that Joseph and Mary were required to offer up for Jesus' birth?

5. What food was to be stored in the ark of the covenant?

• • • • • • • • • •

Total possible points: 1,000
Your score: _____

1. Which of the following animals were considered unclean: cattle, sheep, lizards, weasels, goats, locusts, rabbits, pigeons, camels?

2. What did Jeroboam place in Dan and Bethel for the people to worship?

3. What happened to the scapegoat after it was presented to the Lord?

4. What happened to the thirty pieces of silver after Judas Iscariot threw them back at the Pharisees?

5. What animal did Goliath compare himself to when he saw David approaching him?

• • • • • • • • • • •

Total possible points: 1,500
Your score: _____

1. From what was each gate in the New Jerusalem described in Revelation 21 made?

2. Who dreamed of seven skinny cows eating seven fat cows?

3. What happened to Aaron's golden calf?

4. What bunched herb was to be dipped in blood during the first Passover?

5. What creature of the wilderness does Malachi describe as laying waste to Esau's heritage?

• • • • • • • • • • •

1. What mineral comprised the head of the figure in Nebuchadnezzar's dream?

2. What happened to the bronze serpent that Moses made in the wilderness?

3. What plague in Egypt came first, the frogs or the lice?

4. To what creature did God say, "I will put enmity between you and the woman"?

5. How much gold did the queen of Sheba give Solomon?

• • • • • • • • • • •

Total possible points: 2,500
Your score: _____

Quiz 22

. . . .

Animal, Vegetable, Mineral

Total points for this quiz: 7,500
Your score for this quiz: _____

Running total, Quizzes 1–22: _____

Answers on page 244.

Quiz 23

References and Quotes

People like to quote passages from the Bible—though sometimes they're actually quoting Benjamin Franklin or Mark Twain. The questions that follow will test your real knowledge of scripture.

• • • • • • • • • • •

1. What is the last verse of the Bible?

2. In what book of the Bible can you find "The Lord helps those who help themselves"?

3. When Jesus read in the synagogue, from what book of the Old Testament did He read?

4. According to 1 Corinthians 15:2–4, what is the gospel?

5. Where is the Golden Rule found in the Bible?

• • • • • • • • • • •
Total possible points: 500
Your score: _____

• • • • • • • • • • • •

1. What Bible book says that every thought of man was evil continually?

2. What goes before a fall, per the Proverbs?

3. What does pride go before, again "proverbially"?

4. What are the fruit of the Spirit?

5. What Old Testament minor prophet predicted in his book that the Messiah would be born in Bethlehem?

• • • • • • • • • • •

Total possible points: 1,000
Your score: _____

• • • • • • • • • • •

1. In what book is the following blessing found:
   "The Lord bless you and keep you; the Lord
   make his face shine upon you; the Lord lift
   up His countenance upon you and give you
   peace"?

2. To whom did Jesus say, "Every. . .house divided
   against itself shall not stand"?

3. What two books of the Bible mention the tree
   of life?

4. Who before Jesus referred to the temple as a
   "house of prayer"?

5. What does Psalm 118:24 say we are to do with
   this day the Lord has made?

So...
you think you know the Bible?

• • • • • • • • • • •
Total possible points: 1,500
Your score: _____

1. In Ecclesiastes 12:13, what does the Bible say is the whole duty of man?

2. In Micah 6:8, what does the Lord require of us?

3. What is the first verse of the New Testament?

4. What Old Testament prophet does Peter quote in his speech at Pentecost?

5. What book of the Bible lists the seven deadly sins?

Total possible points: 2,000
Your score: _____

• • • • • • • • • • • •

1. What book of the Bible begins with "How deserted lies the city, once so full of people" (NIV)?

2. According to Genesis 50:20, what did Joseph tell his brothers when they asked his forgiveness?

3. What does the Bible say will happen if you cast your bread upon the waters?

4. What book in the Bible tells us that there is a time to every purpose under heaven, and who was the author of that book?

5. What book contains the only verse in the Bible that mentions the number 666 in connection with a "beast"?

• • • • • • • • • •

Total possible points: 2,500
Your score: _____

Quiz 23

. . . .

References and Quotes

Total points for this quiz: 7,500
Your score for this quiz: _____

Running total, Quizzes 1–23: _____

Answers on page 245.

Quiz 24

Judges

The judges of the Bible weren't like judges today. What can you recall of these mighty "deliverers"?

100 points each

· · · · · · · · · · ·

1. Who was the only woman judge?

2. Did this woman judge preside on a mountain-top, under a palm tree, or in a cave?

3. Why did God tell Barak that a woman would win his battle?

4. What were the people, under Gideon's leadership, to shout when they attacked the Moabites?

5. Who killed Philistines with the jawbone of a donkey?

· · · · · · · · · · ·

Total possible points: 500
Your score: _____

171

• • • • • • • • • • • •

1. What was Gideon's two-part test for God?

2. What test did the angel of the Lord tell Gideon to use to see who was fit to join his army?

3. What judge's mother promised God that if God gave her a son, she would give that son back to God?

4. Who was the first judge of Israel?

5. Who did Samuel make as judges over Israel?

• • • • • • • • • • •

Total possible points: 1,000
Your score: _____

• • • • • • • • • • •

1. What judge used an ox goad to kill six hundred Philistines?

2. What did Samson first suggest to Delilah that she do to find out the secret of his strength?

3. Who was the only judge who sang a victory song?

4. Where was Samson forced to grind as a prisoner of the Philistines?

5. Who was known as the left-handed judge?

• • • • • • • • • • •

Total possible points: 1,500
Your score: _____

• • • • • • • • • • •

1. Which judge stabbed a man who was so fat that his fat closed over the knife?

2. What son of a judge killed all of his brothers except one?

3. Which judge made his own idol for the people to worship?

4. Which judge fought against the Ephraimites after he had just battled the Ammonites?

5. What judge sacrificed his daughter to keep a vow to God?

So... **you think you know the Bible?**

• • • • • • • • • • •

Total possible points: 2,000
Your score: _____

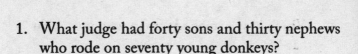

1. What judge had forty sons and thirty nephews who rode on seventy young donkeys?

2. What was the name of Samson's father?

3. What king of Canaan did Barak defeat?

4. Under which judge was the land peaceful for eighty years?

5. Who was judge for six years—the shortest recorded term?

Total possible points: 2,500
Your score: _____

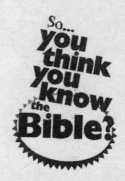

So...
**you
think
you
know
the
Bible?**

Quiz 24

• • • • • • • • • •

Judges

Total points for this quiz: 7,500
Your score for this quiz: _____

Running total, Quizzes 1–24: _____

Answers on page 246.

Quiz 25

Royalty, Part 2

Inspiring, ridiculous, and downright awful—the kings of the Bible were a mixed lot. See if you can separate the wheat from the chaff.

• • • • • • • • • • • •

1. Who was the youngest king of Judah?

2. What king of Israel was described as being head and shoulders above the crowd?

3. Who saved a king's life after he overheard two eunuchs plotting against the king?

4. Why was Israel put into bondage in Egypt?

5. What king of Israel notably had three hundred concubines?

• • • • • • • • • • •
Total possible points: 500
Your score: _____

• • • • • • • • • • • •

1. What king's wife despised him for dancing before the Lord?

2. What king saw the handwriting on the wall?

3. How did King Saul die?

4. What queen did the Ethiopian eunuch in Acts 8 serve?

5. When the golden shields Solomon had made for the temple were stolen, with what did King Rehoboam replace them?

• • • • • • • • • • •

Total possible points: 1,000
Your score: _____

So...
you
think
you
know
the
Bible?

1. Was Zimri king of Israel or Judah?

2. What king lost his mind and lived like a beast of the field?

3. What king was responsible for bringing a guaranteed water supply to Jerusalem?

4. What youngest son of Jehoram was made king of Judah because all of his brothers were killed?

5. What king of Judah cleared the temple of objects used to worship Baal?

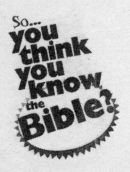

● ● ● ● ● ● ● ● ● ● ●
Total possible points: 1,500
Your score: _____

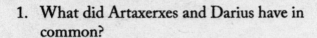
1. What did Artaxerxes and Darius have in common?

2. How long was David king of Judah before he also became king of Israel?

3. How did Omri become king of Israel?

4. What king of Judah was blinded by his captors?

5. Who was the only ruling queen in Judah?

Total possible points: 2,000
Your score: _____

• • • • • • • • • • • •

1. Who was king of Israel for only seven days?

2. Whose reign of fifty-five years was the longest of the kings of Judah?

3. When David was made king of Judah, who was made king of Israel?

4. What king of Israel reigned at the same time as a king of Judah with the same name?

5. Who took away the treasures of Jerusalem during the reign of Rehoboam?

So...
you think you know the Bible?

• • • • • • • • • • •
Total possible points: 2,500
Your score: _____

Quiz 25

• • • • • • • • • • •

Royalty,
Part 2

Total points for this quiz: 7,500
Your score for this quiz: _____

Running total, Quizzes 1–25: _____

Answers on page 247.

Quiz 26

Who's Who, Again

They have gone down in history for their memorable—and sometimes nefarious—deeds. What do you recall about these Bible figures?

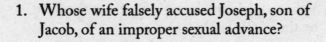

1. Whose wife falsely accused Joseph, son of Jacob, of an improper sexual advance?

2. What wife of King Herod engineered the execution of John the Baptist?

3. Which disciple actually entered the empty tomb?

4. Who rejected Jesus' offer of eternal life because he wouldn't give up what he had?

5. Who was famous for saying, "As for me and my house, we will serve the LORD?"

Total possible points: 500
Your score: _____

• • • • • • • • • •

1. Whose spirit was brought up from the dead by the witch of Endor?

2. To what political party did Jesus' disciple Simon belong?

3. What blind beggar in Jericho received sight from Jesus?

4. Who was born looking red?

5. Whom did Paul accuse of being a hypocrite?

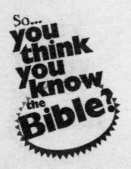

So...
you
think
you
know
the
Bible?

• • • • • • • • • • •
Total possible points: 1,000
Your score: _____

• • • • • • • • • • •

1. What New Testament preacher, like the Old
   Testament hero Samson, was never to drink
   wine or other fermented drink?

2. What sleepy young man fell from an upper
   window and died during a sermon by the
   apostle Paul?

3. Who cursed the day he was born?

4. Who was cursed with sorrow in conception
   and childbirth?

5. What was the name of Timothy's mother?

• • • • • • • • • • •

Total possible points: 1,500
Your score: _____

1. Who was the first recorded Christian martyr?

2. What relative of the late King Saul cursed King David—even throwing dirt on him during Absalom's rebellion?

3. Whom did the people of Lystra insist that Paul and Barnabas were?

4. To whom were the elders referring when, to Boaz, they said Ruth should be as fertile as the two who built the house of Israel?

5. Who stole treasure from the devastated city of Jericho—and paid for his sin with his life?

So...
you
think
you
know
the
Bible?

• • • • • • • • • • •
Total possible points: 2,000
Your score: _____

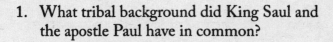

1. What tribal background did King Saul and the apostle Paul have in common?

2. Who used a fable about the king of trees to prove he was supposed to be in charge?

3. Who had the second-longest recorded life-span—962 years?

4. Who was Korah, and what happened to him?

5. To what goddess was Demetrius the silver-smith famous for making shrines?

• • • • • • • • • • •
Total possible points: 2,500
Your score: _____

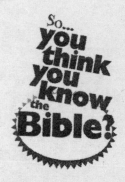

So...
**you
think
you
know
the
Bible?**

Quiz 26

• • • • • • • • • • •

Who's Who, Again

Total points for this quiz: 7,500
Your score for this quiz: _____

Running total, Quizzes 1–26: _____

Answers on page 248.

Quiz 27

Relatives,
Part 2

Here are some more branches on the complicated family trees of the Bible. Can you attach each "twig" to the branch where it belongs?

• • • • • • • • • •

1. What happened to the only son of the widow of Nain?

2. What son was given to Adam and Eve to replace Abel?

3. Who was Samuel's mother?

4. Who was Leah's firstborn?

5. What father and son both wrote psalms?

• • • • • • • • • • •

Total possible points: 500
Your score: _____

1. Who was Orpah's sister-in-law?

2. What was the name of King Saul's cousin who was the commander of his army?

3. Who was King Manasseh's father?

4. Who was the only one of Solomon's children mentioned by name in the Bible?

5. Who was Methuselah's grandson?

• • • • • • • • • • •

Total possible points: 1,000
Your score: _____

• • • • • • • • • •

1. In the Old Testament, what evil person had a wife who was as actively evil as he?

2. Who was David's oldest brother?

3. Which of his brothers did Absalom kill to avenge Tamar's honor?

4. What king of Israel started out good and then let his wives lead him into worship of Ashtoreth and other false gods?

5. What famous leader of Israel married an Ethopian woman?

• • • • • • • • • • •
Total possible points: 1,500
Your score: _____

1. Who killed a whole city of men to avenge their sister's honor?

2. Of what significance was Publius's father to Paul?

3. Whose daughters were said to be the most beautiful in the land?

4. Who was stricken with leprosy because she spoke against her brother's wife?

5. Who was King Saul's father?

• • • • • • • • • • •

Total possible points: 2,000
Your score: _____

1. The ancestors of what two warring nations fought together before they were born?

2. What woman, besides Hannah, was Elkanah's wife?

3. In Mark 6:3, what are the names of Jesus' brothers?

4. What Old Testament man unknowingly slept with his own daughter-in-law—then accused her of being a harlot?

5. When Jacob died, where did his sons bury him?

Total possible points: 2,500
Your score: _____

Quiz 27

· · · · · · · · · · ·

Relatives,
Part 2

Total points for this quiz: 7,500
Your score for this quiz: _____

Running total, Quizzes 1–27: _____

Answers on page 249.

The Lord's Army

Even the least warring among us can be in the Lord's army. Here are both military and nonmilitary Bible characters for you to sort out.

1. Who had to build a wall with one hand while holding his sword in the other?

2. In Ephesians 6, what do we not wrestle against?

3. What military rank did Cornelius, a Gentile convert to Christianity, hold?

4. What kind of shield are we to hold, as described in Ephesians 6?

5. How many were in Gideon's army?

• • • • • • • • • • •
Total possible points: 500
Your score: _____

• • • • • • • • • • •

1. Who said the following, and to whom? "You come against me with sword and spear and javelin, but I come against you in the name of the Lord Almighty, the God of the armies of Israel" (NIV).

2. What did Rahab tell the two spies was the reason she helped them?

3. What kind of headgear does Ephesians 6 say we are to wear?

4. What did Paul tell Timothy to fight?

5. How many stones did David choose from the brook before meeting Goliath?

• • • • • • • • • •

Total possible points: 1,000
Your score: _____

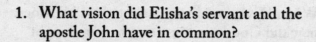

1. What vision did Elisha's servant and the apostle John have in common?

2. Whom did Joshua see right before the battle of Jericho?

3. Who was responsible for taking the ark of the covenant into battle and losing it to the Philistines?

4. According to Peter, how are we to resist our adversary the devil?

5. How did Jesus, by His example in the wilderness, show us to resist Satan?

Total possible points: 1,500
Your score: _____

So...
you think you know the Bible?

• • • • • • • • • • •

1. When David was living among the Philistines, how did God keep him from having to fight against the Israelites?

2. What good king of Judah did Isaiah tell not to worry, that the Lord would fight for him?

3. Who rebuked Sanballat when his army ridiculed the people of the Lord?

4. According to Ephesians 6, what kind of breastplate are we to wear?

5. How many swords did the disciples take with them when they followed Jesus to the Garden of Gethsemane?

So...
you think you know the Bible?

• • • • • • • • • • •
Total possible points: 2,000
Your score: _____

500 points each

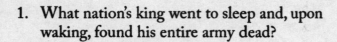

1. What nation's king went to sleep and, upon waking, found his entire army dead?

2. Against what king and people did the Israelites achieve their first victory on their way to the Promised Land?

3. What was the name of the altar that Moses built after the battle where he had to hold up his hands in order for the army to prevail?

4. Why did Joshua lose the first battle against Ai?

5. Whom did Nebuchadnezzar appoint as governor of Judah over the people who remained there?

Total possible points: 2,500
Your score: _____

So... you think you know the Bible?

Quiz 28

· · · · · · · · · · ·

The Lord's Army

Total points for this quiz: 7,500
Your score for this quiz: _____

Running total, Quizzes 1–28: _____

Answers on page 250.

Quiz 29

God's Law

The entire universe operates according to God's laws. See which ones you know.

1. In Matthew 5:17, what did Jesus say He came to do to the law and prophets?

2. What does Numbers 32:23 say will happen if you sin?

3. What does Jesus say keeping God's commandments is proof of?

4. What did God, through His prophet Samuel, say is "better than sacrifice"?

5. On what two commandments did Jesus say hang all the law and the prophets?

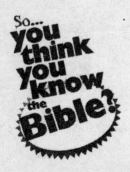

Total possible points: 500
Your score: _____

200 points each

1. What is the first of the Ten Commandments?

2. How many days are we to labor?

3. According to the Ten Commandments, what will happen if we honor our father and mother?

4. What is the first thing listed that we should not covet, per the Ten Commandments?

5. According to Psalm 19, what of the Lord's are true and righteous?

• • • • • • • • • • •

Total possible points: 1,000
Your score: _____

1. What did the people think would happen to them if God, instead of Moses, spoke to them?

2. What kind of stone were the Israelites not to use when building an altar?

3. What psalm mentions the law of the Lord in every verse?

4. What, according to Psalm 19, are God's laws to be desired more than?

5. According to Psalm 1:2, what man does God bless?

· · · · · · · · · · ·

Total possible points: 1,500
Your score: _____

1. Where did Moses tell the Israelites they were to write God's commandments?

2. How long did the unintentional slayer have to stay in the city of refuge?

3. According to Paul, from what curse has Christ redeemed us?

4. To what food does Psalm 19 compare God's Law?

5. What does Galatians 6:2 say we are to do to fulfill the law of Christ?

• • • • • • • • • • •

Total possible points: 2,000
Your score: _____

So...
you
think
you
know
the
Bible?

• • • • • • • • • • •

1. What does God promise in Isaiah 58:13–14 to those who keep His Sabbath?

2. What will we have if, as Joshua 1:8 says, we meditate on the book of the law day and night and do all that is in it?

3. What does Psalm 103:17–18 say is everlasting to those who keep God's covenants?

4. What does James call the law of the Lord?

5. For whom does Paul say the law is not intended?

• • • • • • • • • • •
Total possible points: 2,500
Your score: _____

. . . .

God's Law

Total points for this quiz: 7,500
Your score for this quiz: _____

Running total, Quizzes 1–29: _____

Answers on page 251.

Quiz 30

We Dare You
to Answer These!

For all the Bible brainiacs out there,
this one's for you. Maybe you can even
amaze yourself!

• • • • • • • • • • •

1. Why, according to the King James Version, can it be argued that Shem, Ham, and Japheth were triplets?

2. What was Levirate marriage?

3. What are the colors of the four horses mentioned in Revelation 6?

4. Who were the seven men of honest report mentioned in Acts 6?

5. What people were the Israelites battling on the day the sun stood still?

• • • • • • • • • •

Total possible points: 5,000
Your score: _____

• • • • • • • • • • • •

1. What famous ancestor did the Moabites and Ammonites have in common?

2. Who was Keturah's husband?

3. What was the name of Aaron's wife?

4. What Old Testament man had daughters named Mahlah, Noah, Hoglah, Milcah, and Tirzah—who won the right to inherit his property when he died?

5. From what land were the traders that bought Joseph from his brothers?

• • • • • • • • • • •

Total possible points: 10,000
Your score: _____

1. Who were the fourteen judges of Israel?

2. Who were Jacob's children?

3. What power did the second horseman have in Revelation 6?

4. What grandson of Noah had a name that became symbolic for all those who would try to destroy God's people?

5. Who was Anak?

So...
you
think
you
know
the
Bible?

215

• • • • • • • • • • • •

1. What Old Testament book says, "And the name of the city from that day shall be The LORD Is There"?

2. In what order did the following kings of Israel rule?: Baasha, Pekahiah, Hoshea, Omri, Saul, Joram, Jehu, David, Jeroboam I, Shallum, Jehoahaz, Menahem, Pekah, Ahab, Solomon, Nadab, Zimri, Elah, Ahaziah, Zechariah, Jeroboam II, Jehoash

3. In what order did the following kings of Judah rule?: Josiah, Manasseh, Solomon, Asa, Ahaziah, Rehoboam, Amaziah, Joash, Ahaz, David, Jehoshaphat, Jehoram, Athaliah, Amon, Jehoahaz, Abijah, Azariah, Hezekiah, Zedekiah, Jotham, Jehoiakim, Jehoiachin

4. What group of kings took Lot captive until Abraham rescued him?

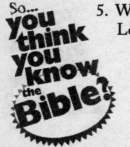

5. What do the wives of Noah, Lot, and Job have in common?

• • • • • • • • • • •

Total possible points: 20,000
Your score: _____

1. What twelve jewels were used in the foundation of the city described in Revelation 21:19–20?

2. What was named Nehushtan?

3. Who was the last person on earth to see the ark of the covenant?

4. What two workmen did God appoint to make the things needed to build the tabernacle and clothe the priests?

5. Who prophesied with a harp?

. . . .
Total possible points: 25,000
Your score: _____

Quiz 30

· · · · · · · · · · · ·

We Dare You
to Answer These!

Total points for this quiz: 75,000
Your score for this quiz: _____

Grand total, Quizzes 1–30: _____

Answers on page 252–253.

A perfect score in
So You Think You Know the Bible
is 292,500 points.

. . . .

How did you fare?

Answer Key

· · · · · · · · · ·

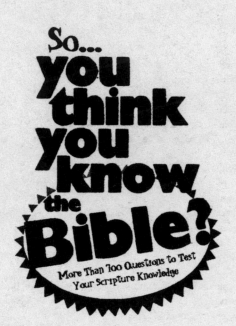

So...
you
think
you
know
the
Bible?

More Than 700 Questions to Test
Your Scripture Knowledge

100

1. Elihu (Job 2:11; 32:2–6)
2. Seven days (Job 2:13)
3. Because they refused to conquer the Promised Land when God told them (Numbers 14)
4. Uzzah (2 Samuel 6:6–7)
5. God and Eve (Genesis 3:11–12)

200

1. Gehazi (2 Kings 5:25–27)
2. Miriam (Exodus 15:20)
3. Aaron, the magicians of Egypt (Exodus 7:8–12)
4. Lucifer (Isaiah 14:12)
5. Phinehas (Numbers 25:7–8)

300

1. Joshua, Hezekiah (Joshua 10:13; 2 Kings 20:11)
2. Take off his sandals, pick up the rod turned into a serpent, put his hand into his bosom (Exodus 3:5; 4:4–7)
3. Smitten with tumors, died (1 Samuel 5:11–12 NIV)
4. Eliezer of Damascus (Genesis 15:2)
5. Eli (1 Samuel 4:16–18)

400

1. She married Salmon and became the mother of Boaz (Matthew 1:5 NIV)
2. Samuel (1 Samuel 7:12)
3. Sisera (Judges 4:17, 21)
4. Leah (Genesis 29:17 NIV)
5. Agag (1 Samuel 15:32)

500

1. Nabal (1 Samuel 25:38)
2. Dagon (1 Samuel 5:3)
3. She nailed a man's head to the ground (Judges 4:21)
4. Enoch—God took him (Genesis 5:24); Elijah—went in a whirlwind to heaven (2 Kings 2:1, 11)
5. The law of Levirate marriage (Deuteronomy 25:5–10; Ruth 4:10, 14)

• • • • • • • • • • • •

100

1. Job (Job 2:9)
2. Terah (Genesis 11:31)
3. Nadab and Abihu (Leviticus 10:1–2)
4. Enoch (Genesis 5:22–29)
5. They were cousins (Esther 2:7)

200

1. Caleb (Judges 3:9)
2. Moses (Exodus 18:1–2)
3. Saul (2 Samuel 9:6)
4. Ahab and Jezebel (1 Kings 19:1–2)
5. James and John (Matthew 4:21–22)

300

1. Isaac (Genesis 24:29)
2. David (Ruth 4:17)
3. Abraham, Isaac (Genesis 12:11–13; 20:1–3; 26:7–11)
4. Appoint seventy men to help him hear all the complaints of the people (Exodus 18)
5. Joab was David's nephew, his sister's son (1 Chronicles 2:12–16; 1 Samuel 26:6)

400

1. Isaiah (Isaiah 8:3)
2. Naomi (Ruth 1:2)
3. David (1 Samuel 18:27; 30:5)
4. They took bribes and perverted justice (1 Samuel 8:3)
5. Rahab (Matthew 1:5 NIV)

500

1. Leah, Rachel, Bilhah, Zilpah (Genesis 29:23–30:24; 35:18)
2. **Leah**: Reuben, Simeon, Levi, Judah, Issachar, Zebulun, Dinah; **Rachel**: Joseph, Benjamin; **Bilhah**: Dan, Naphtali; **Zilpah**: Gad, Asher
3. Three—Nahor, Haran (Genesis 11:27); Sarai (Genesis 20:12)
4. Gideon (Judges 8:29–32)
5. Jephthah (Judges 11:30–31, 34)

100

1. "And who is my neighbor?" (Luke 10:29)
2. The five wise virgins (Matthew 25:8)
3. The last would be first and the first would be last; Jesus would be killed (Matthew 20)
4. The unjust judge (Luke 18:1–8)
5. The prodigal son (Luke 15)

200

1. A man building a tower or a king going into battle, neither of whom had "counted the cost" (Luke 14:26–33)
2. Two men praying at the temple (Luke 18:9–14)
3. Sold all he had and bought it (Matthew 13:46)
4. The unforgiving servant (Matthew 18:22–35)
5. In the talents, the men were given respectively five, two, and one talent; in the pennies/denarii, each man received only one penny/denarius (Matthew 25:15; 20:1–16)

300

1. Nathan (2 Samuel 12)
2. That they didn't deal justly with each other (Isaiah 5:1–7)
3. The rich fool (Luke 12:16–21)
4. Basket, bed (Mark 4:21)
5. Four (Matthew 13:3–8)

400

1. Birds, the sun, thorns (Matthew 13:4–7)
2. The unjust steward (Luke 16:13)
3. To Jericho from Jerusalem (Luke 10:30)
4. The rich man and Lazarus (Luke 16:19–31)
5. The fishing net (Matthew 13:47–50)

500

1. It had been given to the disciples to know the mysteries of the kingdom but not to the general population (Matthew 13:10–11)
2. A stone (Luke 11:11)
3. The kingdom of heaven (Matthew 13:31)
4. The parable of the two sons (Matthew 21:31)
5. The parable of the laborers (Matthew 20:1–16)

100

1. A pair of turtledoves or two young pigeons (Luke 2:24)
2. Twelve (Leviticus 24:5)
3. One (Exodus 25:31)
4. The high priest on the Day of Atonement (Leviticus 16:3, 30–34)
5. He had shed too much blood (1 Chronicles 22:7–8)

200

1. Seven years (1 Kings 6:38)
2. The Lord Himself is the temple (Revelation 21:22)
3. Every day (Exodus 30:7–9)
4. David (1 Chronicles 23–24)
5. The people of Israel, through freewill offerings (Exodus 35:29)

300

1. Almond blossoms (Exodus 37:20)
2. Shittim wood (Exodus 37:25)
3. A veil or curtain (Exodus 26:33)
4. Brass (Exodus 27:19)
5. Zerubbabel (Ezra 3:2)

400

1. Nebuchadnezzar (2 Kings 24:11–14; Jeremiah 52:12–23)
2. By grasping the horns of the altar (1 Kings 1:50)
3. Shiloh (Joshua 18:1)
4. Mount Moriah (2 Chronicles 3:1)
5. Linen (Exodus 26:1) and goats' hair (Exodus 26:7)

500

1. In heaven (Revelation 11:19)
2. In the breastplate (Leviticus 8:8)
3. Fire came down from heaven and consumed the sacrifices; God's glory filled the place (2 Chronicles 7:1)
4. Fourteen (1 Kings 8:65)
5. Asaph (Psalm 50; 1 Chronicles 16:4–6)

100

1. Messiah (Daniel 9:25)
2. Christ (Luke 2:11)
3. Isaac (Genesis 17:19; 18:11–12)
4. Immanuel (Isaiah 7:14)
5. Son of consolation (Acts 4:36)

200

1. Hebrew (Exodus 1:16)
2. Maranatha (1 Corinthians 16:22)
3. Magi (Matthew 2:7 NIV)
4. God Almighty (Exodus 6:3)
5. Abba (Mark 14:36)

300

1. Ecclesiastes (Ecclesiastes 1:1)
2. Bethlehem (Genesis 35:19)
3. Stone of help (1 Samuel 7:12)
4. Nazirite (Judges 13:5)
5. Valley of Hinnom (2 Kings 23:10)

400

1. Most High God (Genesis 14:18)
2. Daniel (Daniel 1:7)
3. Sarah (Genesis 17:16)
4. Mara (Ruth 1:20)
5. Sanhedrin (Matthew 26:59 NIV)

500

1. Maher-shalal-hash-baz (Isaiah 8:1)
2. Benjamin (Genesis 35:18)
3. Malachi (Malachi 1:2–4)
4. "God hath numbered Thy kingdom, and finished it; Thou art weighed in the balances, and art found wanting; Thy kingdom is divided, and given to the Medes and the Persians" (Daniel 5:25–28)
5. Gethsemane (Matthew 26:36, 43)

100

1. Judah (Matthew 1)
2. Levi (Leviticus)
3. Levi (Exodus 2)
4. Matthew—Levi (Mark 2:14)
5. Judah and Benjamin (1 Kings 12:21)

200

1. The tribes of Ephraim and Manasseh (Joshua 16:1–4 NIV)
2. Levi since his father was a priest (Luke 1:5)
3. Gates (Revelation 21:12)
4. Shibboleth (Judges 12:4–6)
5. Rehoboam (1 Kings 12)

300

1. Levi (Joshua 3:6)
2. Dan (Judges 18)
3. East (Numbers 2:3–9)
4. The physical maintenance of the tabernacle and later the temple (Numbers 3:7)
5. As the lost sheep of the house of Israel (Matthew 10:6)

400

1. James (James 1:1)
2. Benjamin (Judges 20:20)
3. Having left-handed men who could sling a stone at a hair's breadth and not miss (Judges 20:16)
4. Manasseh (Deuteronomy 3:13)
5. Ephraim (Isaiah 7:2)

500

1. Dan (Judges 18)
2. 144,000 (Revelation 7:4)
3. Naphtali (Genesis 49:21)
4. Reuben, Gad, and Manasseh (Joshua 18:7)
5. Naphtali (Deuteronomy 33:23)

100

1. Moving upon the face of the waters (Genesis 1:2)
2. Simon the sorcerer (Acts 8:18–19)
3. Comforter (KJV), Counselor (NIV) (John 15:26)
4. By the laying on of hands (Acts 8:17)
5. Paul (2 Timothy 1:6)

200

1. Abide with them forever (John 14:15–17)
2. Jesus' baptism (Matthew 3:16–17)
3. They prophesied (Numbers 11:25)
4. This world (1 Corinthians 2:12)
5. His children (Romans 8:16)

300

1. Strive with men (Genesis 6:3)
2. Water (John 7:38–39), wind (John 3:8), seal (Ephesians 1:13), dove (Matthew 3:16), fire (Acts 2:3)
3. Dream dreams, prophesy (Joel 2:28–32; Acts 2:16–21)
4. That Paul would be bound by the Jews in Jerusalem and delivered to the Gentiles (Acts 21:11)
5. The lust of the flesh (Galatians 5:16)

400

1. Makes intercession for us (Romans 8:26)
2. Caught him away (Acts 8:39)
3. Power, love, and a sound mind (2 Timothy 1:7)
4. As foolishness (1 Corinthians 2:14)
5. He breathed on them (John 20:22)

500

1. The promised Holy Spirit (Ephesians 1:13)
2. Doctrine, reproof, correction, instruction in righteousness (2 Timothy 3:16)
3. Quench Him (1 Thessalonians 5:19)
4. With the bond of peace (Ephesians 4:3)
5. Test the spirits (1 John 4:1–3)

100
1. Satan (2 Corinthians 11:14)
2. Chief prince (Daniel 10:13)
3. Twice (Genesis 22:10–18)
4. Manna (Psalm 78:24–25)
5. Balaam's donkey (Numbers 22:23)

200
1. Jesus (Luke 10:18)
2. They brought him and his family out of Sodom and told him to flee (Genesis 19:16, 22)
3. Joseph (Matthew 1:20)
4. Cornelius (Acts 10:3)
5. Some apostles (Acts 5:19)

300
1. To stand watch over the sons of Daniel's people (Daniel 12:1)
2. All those who fear the Lord (Psalm 34:7)
3. Herod (Acts 12:23)
4. The apostles (1 Corinthians 4:9)
5. Christians (1 Corinthians 6:3)

400
1. Satan (Ezekiel 28:12–14 NIV)
2. Jude (Jude 9) and Revelation (Revelation 12:7)
3. Jacob (Israel) (Genesis 48:16)
4. An old prophet who lived in Bethel (1 Kings 13:18)
5. The angel of His presence (Isaiah 63:9)

500
1. Daniel (Daniel 8:16), Zacharias (Luke 1:19), Mary (Luke 1:26)
2. Guardians of Eden and the tree of life (Genesis 3:24)
3. One set to fly with, one set to cover their faces, one set to cover their feet (Isaiah 6:2)
4. Gideon (Judges 6:22–23)
5. David (1 Samuel 29:9)

1. An ephod (Exodus 28:6–14)
2. Zadok (1 Kings 1:39)
3. Anointing, consecrating, and sanctifying (Exodus 28:41)
4. Ezra (Ezra 7:11)
5. Melchizedek (Genesis 14:18)

200

1. Almond (Numbers 17:8)
2. Day of Atonement (Leviticus 16; 23:26–32)
3. Bells (Exodus 28:33–34)
4. Peter (1 Peter 2:5, 9)
5. Jeroboam (1 Kings 13:33)

300

1. Jehoiada (2 Kings 11:1–4)
2. Eli (1 Samuel 4:11)
3. A gold plate was engraved with HOLINESS TO THE LORD (Exodus 28:36)
4. Jehu (2 Kings 10:11)
5. Hilkiah (2 Kings 22:8)

400

1. Caiaphas (John 11:50)
2. Joseph's wife (Genesis 41:45)
3. Thirteen (Joshua 21:19)
4. Ananias (Acts 23:2–3)
5. Saul (1 Samuel 13:8–14)

500

1. Abijah (Luke 1:5 NIV)
2. Ahimelech (1 Samuel 21:6)
3. Trying to cast out evil spirits (Acts 19:14–16)
4. Urijah (2 Kings 16:11)
5. The Sheep Gate (Nehemiah 3:1)

100
1. That He would make Abram's name great and through him all nations would be blessed (Genesis 12:2–3)
2. Zechariah (Zechariah 11:12–13)
3. Micah (Micah 5:2)
4. Joseph fled to Egypt with Mary and Jesus to escape Herod (Matthew 2:15)
5. David (Psalm 22:14)

200
1. They will be slaves of Japheth's and Shem's descendants (Genesis 9:25–27)
2. Not one stone would be left upon another (Matthew 24:2)
3. John the Baptist (Isaiah 40:3; Malachi 3:1)
4. The four world empires to come (Daniel 7)
5. Jonah (Matthew 12:39–40)

300
1. That Messiah would be a descendant of Judah (Genesis 49:8–12)
2. That God would restore His people to their land (Ezekiel 37:11–14)
3. Cyrus (Ezra 1:1–3)
4. After the Holy Spirit came upon them (Acts 1:8)
5. Isaiah 53

400
1. Twelve (Genesis 17:20)
2. Joel (Joel 2:28–29)
3. Dust (Genesis 28:14)
4. The days of Noah (Matthew 24:37)
5. The man from Macedonia (Acts 16:9)

500
1. The mountain will split in two (Zechariah 14:4)
2. They bowed down to him (Genesis 37:9–11)
3. Judas Iscariot (Psalm 41:9; Acts 1:16)
4. The queen of the south, the men of Nineveh (Matthew 12:41–42)
5. A great famine throughout the world (Acts 11:28)

100

1. Three (Habakkuk)
2. Seven (Genesis 8:10)
3. Abraham was one hundred, Sarah was ninety (Genesis 21:5; 17:17)
4. Twenty—ten were killed and he had ten more (Job 1:2; 42:13)
5. One of each (Genesis 6:16)

200

1. Solomon (1 Kings 11:3)
2. Eighty-six (Genesis 16:16)
3. Fifty cubits (Esther 5:14)
4. Forty days and forty nights (Exodus 24:18)
5. Not a single one (Matthew 6:27)

300

1. About three thousand (Acts 2:41)
2. Seventy (Exodus 1:5)
3. Two (Ruth 1:2)
4. Ten (Daniel 1:12)
5. Twelve (Luke 2:42–43)

400

1. Fourteen (Twelve in the book of Judges, plus Eli [1 Samuel 4:15–18] and Samuel [1 Samuel 17:6])
2. Seven thousand (1 Kings 19:18)
3. 969 (Genesis 5:27)
4. Seventy (Luke 10:1)
5. Four (Exodus 39:10)

500

1. Obadiah, Philemon, 2 John, 3 John, Jude
2. 180 days (Esther 1:4)
3. Six hundred years old (Genesis 7:6)
4. Seven months (1 Samuel 6:1)
5. Twenty years (1 Samuel 7:2)

100

• • • • • • • • • • •

1. Saul, later known as Paul (Acts 7:58)
2. Searching the scriptures (Acts 17:11)
3. Paul (Romans 1:1)
4. James (Matthew 10:3; Luke 6:16; Matthew 13:55)
5. Peter (Acts 9:36–43) and Paul (Acts 20:9–10)

200

1. Onesimus (Philemon 1:10)
2. Andrew (John 6:8–9)
3. Barnabas (Acts 13:2), Silas (Acts 15:40), Timothy (Acts 16:1–3)
4. Apollos (Acts 18:24–28)
5. Ananias (Acts 9:10–18)

300

1. Matthias (Acts 1:26)
2. Timothy (Acts 16:3), Titus (Galatians 2:3)
3. Robbery (John 18:40), insurrection/sedition, and murder (Mark 15:7; Luke 23:18–19)
4. Stephen (Acts 6:15)
5. Two (Matthew 27:5; Acts 1:18)

400

1. Rhoda (Acts 12:13)
2. Peter (2 Peter 3:15)
3. He was a thief (John 12:4–6)
4. Legion (Mark 5:9)
5. James and John (Matthew 20:20; Mark 10:35)

500

1. Simon Peter (John 1:40); Simon, a brother of Jesus (Mark 6:3); Simon the Zealot, one of the disciples (Acts 1:13); Simon the leper (Matthew 26:6); Simon of Cyrene (Matthew 27:32); Simon the sorcerer (Acts 8:9); Simon the Pharisee (Luke 7:36, 40); Simon Iscariot, Judas's father (John 6:71); Simon the tanner (Acts 9:43)
2. Crispus and Gaius (1 Corinthians 1:14)
3. Demetrius (Acts 19:24)
4. To make sure the Greek widows were provided for (Acts 6:1–3)
5. Euodias and Syntyche (Philippians 4:2)

• • • • • • • • • •

100
1. Herding sheep (Exodus 3:1)
2. Simon Peter (Luke 5:1–10; John 21:2–4)
3. Tentmakers (Acts 18:3)
4. The lords of the Philistines (Judges 16:4–5)
5. Treasurer (Acts 8:27)

200
1. Baker and butler (cupbearer) (Genesis 40)
2. Governor of Judea (Luke 3:1)
3. Matthew (Matthew 9:9–13) and Zacchaeus (Luke 19:1–10)
4. Witch of Endor (1 Samuel 28:7–8)
5. Felix and Festus (Acts 24:27)

300
1. Nehemiah (Nehemiah 1:11–2:1)
2. Second only to Pharaoh (Genesis 41:40)
3. His wife's slave girl (2 Kings 5:2)
4. Shepherds (Genesis 4:2; 29:9; Exodus 2:16)
5. Brass and iron (Genesis 4:22)

400
1. Shepherd (Amos 1:1)
2. Physician (Colossians 4:14)
3. Captain of the guard (Genesis 39:1)
4. Schoolmaster (tutor) (Galatians 3:24)
5. Publican (tax collector) (Luke 18:10)

500
1. Gedaliah (Jeremiah 40:5)
2. He set them over the affairs of the province of Babylon (Daniel 3:12)
3. He was servant to Elah who was king of Israel before him (1 Kings 16:9)
4. Reuel (Jethro) (Exodus 2:16–18)
5. They were both prophetesses (2 Chronicles 34:22; Luke 2:36)

100

1. The creation (Romans 1:20)
2. I AM THAT I AM (Exodus 3:14)
3. Moses (Exodus 32:9–14)
4. Six days (Genesis 1:31)
5. In spirit and in truth (John 4:24)

200

1. David (1 Samuel 13:14; Acts 13:22)
2. Abraham (James 2:23)
3. Diligently keeping God's commands (Exodus 15:26)
4. The magi (Matthew 2:7–12)
5. The heavens (Psalm 19:1)

300

1. When He saw that every thought of man was evil continually (Genesis 6:5–8)
2. In the new heaven and new earth (Revelation 21:4)
3. So God can be magnified and David can speak of His righteousness all the day long (Psalm 35:27–28)
4. Job (Job 1:6)
5. Hagar (Genesis 16:13 NIV)

400

1. Baptism (Matthew 3:16–17); transfiguration (Mark 9:1–7)
2. As yesterday, or a day (Psalm 90:4)
3. "Hear, O Israel: The LORD our God is one LORD" (Deuteronomy 6:4)
4. Condemn the world (John 3:17)
5. The ground (Genesis 3:17)

500

1. Enoch (Genesis 5:24)
2. Mighty wind, earthquake, fire (1 Kings 19:11–12)
3. A proud look, a lying tongue, hands that shed innocent blood, a heart that devises wicked plans, feet that are swift in running to evil, a false witness who speaks lies, and one who sows discord among brethren (Proverbs 6:15–19)
4. The firstborn (Exodus 13:2)
5. He rejoices over us with singing (Zephaniah 3:17)

100

1. James and John (Mark 3:17)
2. Feast of Unleavened Bread (Exodus 23:15)
3. David (1 Samuel 16:18, 23)
4. John the Baptist (Matthew 3:4)
5. Bathsheba (Matthew 1:6; 2 Samuel 11:3; 2 Samuel 12:24)

200

1. Ben-oni (Genesis 35:18)
2. Hadassah (Esther 2:7)
3. His name was changed to *Israel* (Genesis 32:28)
4. Matthew (Matthew 10:3; Mark 2:14)
5. Paul (Ephesians 6:20)

300

1. Noah (Genesis 6:8)
2. Shadrach, Meshach, and Abednego (Daniel 1:7)
3. The field of blood (Matthew 27:7–8)
4. The great dragon, that old serpent (Revelation 12:9)
5. Joseph (Genesis 41:45)

400

1. Belteshazzar (Daniel 1:7)
2. Mara (Ruth 1:20)
3. Jesus (Hebrews 12:2)
4. The two pillars in front of the temple (2 Chronicles 3:17)
5. Gideon (Judges 7:1)

500

1. Nimrod (Genesis 10:9)
2. Jabal (Genesis 4:20)
3. The ten spies who gave a bad report (Numbers 13)
4. Jerusalem (Judges 19:10)
5. The name of a storm (Acts 27:14)

100
1. Elisha (2 Kings 4:18–37)
2. Four (Isaiah 1:1)
3. Eat unclean food (Daniel 1:8)
4. Moses (Numbers 12:6–8)
5. Isaiah (Isaiah 6:6–7)

200
1. Amos (Amos 1:1) and Micah (Micah 1:1) [Isaiah 1:1]
2. Baruch (Jeremiah 36:4, 17–18)
3. Daniel (Daniel 4:25)
4. Amos (Amos 3:3)
5. Ezekiel (Ezekiel 2:9–3:3)

300
1. Jehoiakim (Jeremiah 36:9–26)
2. Philip the evangelist (Acts 21:8–9)
3. Ezekiel (Ezekiel 48:30–35)
4. Elisha (2 Kings 13:20–21)
5. Hosea (Hosea 1:6, 9 NIV)

400
1. Solomon (1 Kings 1:34)
2. A lion killed him (1 Kings 13:20–24)
3. Saul (1 Samuel 9:27; 10:6)
4. Jonah (Jonah 4:3)
5. Daniel (Matthew 24:15)

500
1. Micaiah (1 Kings 22:15–18)
2. 390 days (Ezekiel 4:4–5)
3. Hosea (Hosea 1:2)
4. Edom (Obadiah 1:1)
5. Hananiah (Jeremiah 28)

100

1. Ahab and Jezebel (1 Kings 21)
2. Jehu (2 Kings 9:20)
3. Vashti (Esther 1:11)
4. Melchizedek (Genesis 14:17–20)
5. Ahab (1 Kings 16:30)

200

1. Killed all her grandchildren so she could be queen (2 Kings 11:1)
2. King Hiram of Tyre (2 Chronicles 2:3, 8)
3. Nebuchadnezzar (2 Kings 24)
4. Herod: Herod the Great (Matthew 2:1–20), Herod Antipas (Mark 8:15), Herod Agrippa I (Acts 12), Herod Agrippa II (Acts 25)
5. Saul (1 Samuel 28:7–25)

300

1. Because He was pleased that Solomon asked for wisdom (2 Chronicles 1:11–12)
2. Absalom (2 Samuel 18:1–18)
3. Balak (Numbers 22)
4. Samuel (1 Samuel 8:6–7)
5. Darius (Daniel 5:31; 6:16–23)

400

1. Hoshea (2 Kings 18:9–11)
2. Zedekiah (2 Chronicles 36:10)
3. Shalmaneser (2 Kings 17:3, 6)
4. Adonijah (1 Kings 2:23–25)
5. Tetrarch of Galilee (Luke 3:1)

500

1. Jeroboam II (2 Kings 13:13)
2. Agag (1 Samuel 15:8–9)
3. Jeroboam I (1 Kings 13:4)
4. She was thrown out a window and dogs devoured her in the street (2 Kings 9:32–36)
5. Moabites (Numbers 22)

100

1. His mother and her sister Mary (wife of Cleophas) and Mary Magdalene (John 19:25)
2. Pharisees and scribes (Matthew 15:1, 14)
3. Simeon (Luke 2:25–26)
4. Mary Magdalene (John 20:1, 11–15)
5. "There is none good but...God" (Mark 10:18)

200

1. Satan (Matthew 4:4)
2. Andrew (John 1:40)
3. Augustus (Luke 2:1)
4. Feast of Passover (Luke 2:41)
5. Three days (Luke 2:46)

300

1. Tamar, Rahab, Ruth, Bathsheba ("Uriah's wife") (Matthew 1 NIV)
2. Mount of Olives (Matthew 24:3)
3. He healed a man's withered hand (Mark 3:1–5)
4. The chief priests and elders (Matthew 26:14–16)
5. "Hosanna to the son of David: Blessed is he that cometh in the name of the Lord" (Matthew 21:9)

400

1. "The baptism of John, whence was it? From heaven or of men?" (Matthew 21:24–25)
2. As the spiritual Rock that followed them (1 Corinthians 10:4)
3. Four days (John 11:17)
4. Joseph of Arimathea and Nicodemus (John 19:38–42)
5. "Father, into thy hands I commend my spirit" (Luke 23:46)

500

1. Bread of Life (John 6:35); Light of the World (John 8:12); Door (John 10:7); Good Shepherd (John 10:11); the Way, the Truth, the Life (John 14:6)
2. A just or innocent man (Matthew 27:19)
3. John the Baptist (John 1:29)
4. Power and authority over all demons and to cure diseases (Luke 9:1)
5. Jeroboam, Saul, Daniel (Matthew 1)

100 • • • • • • • • • •

1. Mount Carmel (1 Kings 18:19)
2. Abraham (Hebrews 11:8)
3. Tarshish (Jonah 1:3)
4. Ur of the Chaldeans (Genesis 11:31)
5. Wilderness of Paran (Numbers 13:3)

200

1. Gaza (Judges 16:1–3)
2. Babel (Genesis 11:9)
3. Babylon (Ezekiel 1:3 NIV)
4. On the lower slopes of the Mount of Olives (Matthew 26:30–36; Mark 14:26–32)
5. Bethany (John 11:1)

300

1. Midian (Exodus 2:15)
2. Damascus (Acts 9:19–25)
3. By the Sheep Gate in Jerusalem—an angel stirred up the water, and the first one in after that would be healed (John 5:2–4)
4. The four rivers that flowed out of the Garden of Eden (Genesis 2:10–14)
5. Emmaus (Luke 24:13)

400

1. Egypt (Jeremiah 43:7–8)
2. In the center (Genesis 2:9; 3:6)
3. Standing right next to her (Genesis 3:6)
4. Nineveh (Genesis 10:11–12 NIV; Jonah 3:3)
5. Mount Nebo (Deuteronomy 32:48–49)

500

1. In the land of Moab (Deuteronomy 34:6)
2. Corinth (Acts 18:1–2)
3. He died and was buried there (Numbers 20:25–28)
4. Bethany (Luke 24:50)
5. Jehovah-jireh: The Lord will provide (Genesis 22:14)

Quiz 20: Meanings of Words, Part 2

100

1. Solomon (1 Kings 10:1)
2. Apostles (Revelation 21:14)
3. Sabbath (Mark 2:27)
4. Eve (Genesis 4:25)
5. The place of the skull (Matthew 27:33)

200

1. Deuteronomy (Deuteronomy 34:5–8)
2. Ruth (Matthew 1:5)
3. Samaria (John 4:9)
4. Barabbas (Mark 15:15)
5. Bethel (Genesis 35:1)

300

1. Wormwood (Revelation 8:10–11)
2. Abaddon or Apollyon (Revelation 9:11)
3. Jemima (Job 42:14)
4. Belial (Deuteronomy 13:13)
5. Jacob (Genesis 25:28)

400

1. A gift or offering (Mark 7:11)
2. Pur (Esther 3:7))
3. Rahab (Joshua 2:1, 15, 18)
4. Baal (Judges 6:25)
5. Ashtoreth (1 Kings 11:5)

500

1. Babylon (2 Kings 20:12)
2. Elijah (1 Kings 17:1)
3. Elisha (2 Kings 2:19–22)
4. Felix (Acts 24:25)
5. Meribah (Exodus 17:7)

100

1. The prayers of the saints (Revelation 8:3–4)
2. Paying taxes (Matthew 22:17–21)
3. Chosen (Matthew 22:14)
4. Wool (Isaiah 1:18)
5. First day (Exodus 12:15)

200

1. Cymbals (Psalm 150:5)
2. His wife (Job 2:9)
3. The seas (Genesis 1:10), as opposed to stars (Genesis 1:16)
4. Feast of the New Moon (1 Samuel 20:5)
5. One God and Father (Ephesians 4:6)

300

1. Gopher wood (Genesis 6:14)
2. Mint, anise, and cummin (cumin) (Matthew 23:23)
3. Buzi (Ezekiel 1:3)
4. Feast of Ingathering (Booths) (Exodus 23:16)
5. In Philippi (Acts 16:12–14)

400

1. The flood (Genesis 6)
2. Every fifty years (Leviticus 25:10)
3. The kinsman gave Boaz his sandal (Ruth 4:7–8)
4. Because Claudius commanded all the Jews to leave Rome (Acts 18:1–2)
5. Athens (Acts 17:22–23)

500

1. Ephesus, Smyrna, Pergamos, Thyatira, Sardis, Philadelphia, Laodicea (Revelation 2–3)
2. Under a tree at Jabesh (1 Samuel 31:12–13)
3. A penny (denarius NIV) (Matthew 22:17–21)
4. A Sabbath day's journey (Acts 1:12)
5. Epicureans and Stoics (Acts 17:18)

100

1. Bear, lion (1 Samuel 17:34)
2. Seven (Genesis 7:2)
3. Quail (Exodus 16:13)
4. Lamb of God (John 1:29)
5. The prodigal son (Luke 15:23)

200

1. A vineyard (Genesis 9:20)
2. Sycamore (Luke 19:4)
3. Lion, calf (ox NIV), man, eagle (Revelation 4:7)
4. Two turtledoves or two young pigeons (Luke 2:24)
5. Pot of manna (Exodus 16:32–34)

300

1. Lizards, weasels, rabbits, camels (Leviticus 11)
2. Two golden calves (1 Kings 12:28–29)
3. It was released to the wilderness (Leviticus 16:7–10, 21–22)
4. They were used to buy a potter's field (Matthew 27:7)
5. Dog (1 Samuel 17:43)

400

1. Single pearl (Revelation 21:21)
2. Pharaoh (Genesis 41)
3. It was ground into powder and mixed with water, and the people were forced to drink it (Exodus 32:20)
4. Hyssop (Exodus 12:22)
5. Dragons (Malachi 1:3)

500

1. Fine gold (Daniel 2:32–33)
2. King Hezekiah destroyed it by the order of God (2 Kings 18:4)
3. Frogs (Exodus 8:5–17)
4. The serpent (Genesis 3:14–15)
5. 120 talents (1 Kings 10:10)

100

1. "The grace of our Lord Jesus Christ be with you all. Amen." (Revelation 22:21)
2. Trick question—it isn't in the Bible
3. Isaiah (Luke 4:17–18)
4. That, according to the scriptures, Jesus died for our sins, was buried, and rose again on the third day (1 Corinthians 15:2–4)
5. Matthew 7:12

200

1. Genesis (Genesis 6:5)
2. A haughty spirit (Proverbs 16:18)
3. Destruction (Proverbs 16:18)
4. Love, joy, peace, longsuffering, gentleness, goodness, faith, meekness, temperance (Galatians 5:22–23)
5. Micah (Micah 5:2)

300

1. Numbers (Numbers 6:24–26)
2. The Pharisees (Matthew 12:24–25)
3. Genesis and Revelation (Genesis 2:9, 3:22, 3:24; Revelation 2:7, 22:14)
4. Isaiah (Isaiah 56:7)
5. Rejoice and be glad in it (Psalm 118:24)

400

1. Fear God and keep His commandments (Ecclesiastes 12:13)
2. To do justly, to love mercy, and to walk humbly with your God (Micah 6:8)
3. "The book of the generation of Jesus Christ, the son of David, the son of Abraham." (Matthew 1:1)
4. Joel (Acts 2:16)
5. None—they're not in the Bible

500

1. Lamentations (Lamentations 1:1)
2. "You meant it for evil but God meant it for good" (Genesis 50:20, paraphrase)
3. You will find it after many days (Ecclesiastes 11:1)
4. Ecclesiastes, Solomon (Ecclesiastes 3:1)
5. Revelation (Revelation 13:18)

100

1. Deborah (Judges 4)
2. Under a palm tree (Judges 4:5)
3. Because Barak refused to go to battle unless Deborah came with him (Judges 4:8–9)
4. "The sword of the LORD and of Gideon" (Judges 7:18)
5. Samson (Judges 15:16)

200

1. Fleece wet, ground dry; fleece dry, ground wet (Judges 6:36–40)
2. Let them drink water; only keep the ones who lap the water from their hands (Judges 7:5)
3. Samuel (1 Samuel 1:11)
4. Othniel (Judges 3:9)
5. His sons (1 Samuel 8:1)

300

1. Shamgar (Judges 3:31)
2. Bind him with seven fresh cords/thongs, not yet dried (Judges 16:8)
3. Deborah (Judges 5)
4. Gaza (Judges 16:21)
5. Ehud (Judges 3:15)

400

1. Ehud (Judges 3:22)
2. Abimelech (Judges 9)
3. Gideon (Judges 8:27)
4. Jephthah (Judges 12)
5. Jephthah (Judges 11:30–40)

500

1. Abdon (Judges 12:13–14)
2. Manoah (Judges 13)
3. Jabin (Judges 4)
4. Ehud (Judges 3:26–30)
5. Jephthah (Judges 12:7)

100   ● ● ● ● ● ● ● ● ● ● ● ●

1. Joash was seven years old when he became king (2 Kings 11)
2. Saul (1 Samuel 9:2)
3. Mordecai (Esther 2:21–23)
4. There arose a pharaoh who didn't know Joseph (Exodus 1:8)
5. Solomon (1 Kings 11:3)

200

1. David (2 Samuel 6:16)
2. Belshazzar (Daniel 5)
3. He deliberately fell on a sword (1 Samuel 31:4)
4. Candace (Acts 8:27)
5. Bronze shields (1 Kings 14:27)

300

1. Israel (1 Kings 16:16)
2. Nebuchadnezzar (Daniel 4:32–33)
3. Hezekiah (2 Kings 20:20; 2 Chronicles 32:30)
4. Ahaziah (2 Chronicles 22:1)
5. Josiah (2 Kings 23:4)

400

1. They were rulers of Persia while Jerusalem was being rebuilt after the return from Babylonian exile (Ezra 4, 6)
2. Seven years, six months (2 Samuel 5:5)
3. Zimri, who was king, killed himself (1 Kings 16:18), and Tibni, Omri's rival, died (1 Kings 16:22)
4. Zedekiah (Jeremiah 39:7)
5. Athaliah (2 Chronicles 22:10–12)

500

1. Zimri (1 Kings 16:15)
2. Manasseh (2 Kings 21)
3. Ishbosheth (2 Samuel 2:10)
4. Jehoash (2 Kings 13:10–11; 2 Kings 12:2)
5. Shishak, king of Egypt (1 Kings 14:25)

100

1. Potiphar (Genesis 39)
2. Herodias (Mark 6:14–29)
3. Peter (John 20:6)
4. Rich young ruler (Matthew 19:22)
5. Joshua (Joshua 24:15)

200

1. Samuel (1 Samuel 28:7–25)
2. He was a Zealot (Luke 6:15; Acts 1:13)
3. Bartimaeus (Mark 10:46–52)
4. Esau (Genesis 25:25)
5. Peter (Galatians 2:11–14)

300

1. John the Baptist (Judges 13:5; Luke 1:13–15)
2. Eutychus (Acts 20:7–12)
3. Job (Job 3:1)
4. Eve (Genesis 3:16–20)
5. Eunice (2 Timothy 1:5)

400

1. Stephen (Acts 7:54)
2. Shimei (2 Samuel 16)
3. Jupiter and Mercurius (Zeus and Hermes NIV) (Acts 14:12)
4. Leah and Rachel (Ruth 4:11)
5. Achan (Joshua 7)

500

1. Benjamin (1 Samuel 9:1; Philippians 3:5)
2. Abimelech (Judges 9)
3. Jared (Genesis 5:20)
4. He led a rebellion against Moses and Aaron and was swallowed by the earth (Numbers 16)
5. Diana (Acts 19:24)

100

1. He was raised from the dead by Jesus (Luke 7:11–15)
2. Seth (Genesis 4:25)
3. Hannah (1 Samuel 1:9–11)
4. Reuben (Genesis 29:32)
5. David and Solomon (Psalm 62; 72)

200

1. Ruth (Ruth 1:14–15)
2. Abner (1 Samuel 14:50)
3. Hezekiah (2 Kings 21:1–3)
4. Rehoboam (1 Kings 11:43)
5. Noah (Genesis 5:25–29)

300

1. Ahab (1 Kings 19:1–2)
2. Eliab (1 Samuel 17:28)
3. Amnon (2 Samuel 13:28–29)
4. Solomon (1 Kings 11:4–5)
5. Moses (Numbers 12:1)

400

1. Simeon and Levi (Genesis 34:25)
2. Paul healed him of a fever (Acts 28:7–8)
3. Job (Job 42:15)
4. Miriam (Numbers 12:10)
5. Kish (1 Samuel 9:1)

500

1. Israelites (Jacob) and Edomites (Esau) (Genesis 25:21–26)
2. Peninnah (1 Samuel 1:2)
3. James, Joses, Juda, and Simon (Mark 6:3)
4. Judah (Genesis 38)
5. In the cave Abraham bought for a burial place (Genesis 50:13)

QUIZ 28: THE LORD'S ARMY

100

1. Nehemiah (Nehemiah 4:17–18)
2. Flesh and blood (Ephesians 6:12)
3. Centurion (Acts 10:1)
4. Shield of faith (Ephesians 6:16)
5. Three hundred (Judges 7:6–7)

200

1. David to Goliath (1 Samuel 17:45)
2. She had heard that their God fought for them (Joshua 2:10)
3. Helmet of salvation (Ephesians 6:17)
4. The good fight of faith (1 Timothy 6:12)
5. Five smooth stones (1 Samuel 17:40)

300

1. They both saw the spiritual army of the Lord (2 Kings 6:15–17; Revelation 12:7)
2. The commander of the Lord's army (Joshua 5:14)
3. The elders of Israel (1 Samuel 4:3)
4. By standing steadfast in the faith (1 Peter 5:9)
5. He quoted scriptures to him (Matthew 4:1–11)

400

1. God turned the lords of the Philistines against David, and they wouldn't let him go with them to fight (1 Samuel 29:9)
2. Hezekiah (2 Kings 19:32–34)
3. Nehemiah (Nehemiah 6)
4. Breastplate of righteousness (Ephesians 6:14)
5. Two (Luke 22:38)

500

1. Assyria (2 Kings 19:35–36; Isaiah 37:36–37)
2. Sihon, Amorites (Numbers 21:21–31)
3. Jehovahnissi—The Lord Is My Banner (Exodus 17:15)
4. Because Israel had sinned (Joshua 7:11)
5. Gedaliah (2 Kings 25:22–23)

100

1. Fulfill them (Matthew 5:17)
2. You will be found out (Numbers 32:23)
3. Loving Him (John 14:15)
4. Obedience (1 Samuel 15:22)
5. "Thou shalt love the Lord thy God with all thy heart, and with all thy soul, and with all thy mind" and "Thou shalt love thy neighbor as thyself" (Matthew 22:37, 39)

200

1. "Thou shalt have no other gods before me" (Exodus 20:3)
2. Six (Exodus 20:9)
3. Your days will be long (Exodus 20:12)
4. Neighbor's house (Exodus 20:17)
5. Judgments (Psalm 19:9)

300

1. They would die (Exodus 20:19)
2. Hewn stone (Exodus 20:25)
3. Psalm 119
4. Much fine gold (Psalm 19:10)
5. One whose delight is in the law of the Lord (Psalm 1:2)

400

1. On their doorposts (Deuteronomy 6:9)
2. Until he stood before the congregation for judgment and until the death of the one who was high priest at that time (Joshua 20:6)
3. Curse of the law (Galatians 3:13)
4. Honey (Psalm 19:7–10)
5. Bear one another's burdens (Galatians 6:2)

500

1. They would find joy in the Lord (Isaiah 58:13–14)
2. A prosperous way and good success (Joshua 1:8)
3. His mercy (Psalm 103:17–18)
4. The perfect law of liberty (James 1:25)
5. The righteous (1 Timothy 1:9)

1,000

1. Because it indicates they were born when "Noah was five hundred years old" (Genesis 5:32)
2. If a man died without children, his brother was required to have a child with the widow, and that child would be considered the child of the man who had died (Deuteronomy 25:5–10)
3. White, fiery red, black, pale (Revelation 6)
4. Stephen, Philip, Procorus, Nicanor, Timon, Parmenas, Nicolas (Acts 6:5)
5. Amorites (Joshua 10:12–14)

2,000

1. Lot (Genesis 19:35–38)
2. Abraham (Genesis 25:1)
3. Elisheba (Exodus 6:23)
4. Zelophehad (Numbers 27:1–11)
5. Midian (Genesis 37:28)

3,000

1. Othniel, Ehud, Shamgar, Deborah, Gideon, Tola, Jair, Jephthah, Ibzan, Elon, Abdon, Samson, Samuel, Eli (Judges and 1 Samuel)
2. Reuben, Asher, Simeon, Issachar, Gad, Judah, Joseph, Levi, Benjamin, Zebulun, Naphtali, Dan, Dinah (Genesis 29–30, 35)
3. Power to take peace from the earth (Revelation 6:4)
4. Magog (Genesis 10:2; Ezekiel 38)
5. The ancestor of the giants in the land of Canaan (Numbers 13:33)

4,000

1. Ezekiel (Ezekiel 48:35)
2. Saul, David, Solomon, Jeroboam I, Nadab, Baasha, Elah, Zimri, Omri, Ahab, Ahaziah, Joram, Jehu, Jehoahaz, Jehoash, Jeroboam II, Zechariah, Shallum, Menahem, Pekahiah, Pekah, Hoshea (1 and 2 Kings and 1 and 2 Chronicles)
3. David, Solomon, Rehoboam, Abijah, Asa, Jehoshaphat, Jehoram, Ahaziah, Athaliah, Joash, Amaziah, Azariah, Jotham, Ahaz, Hezekiah, Manasseh, Amon, Josiah, Jehoahaz, Jehoiakim, Jehoiachin, Zedekiah (1 and 2 Kings and 1 and 2 Chronicles)

4. Amraphel, king of Shinar; Arioch, king of Ellasar; Chedorlaomer, king of Elam; and Tidal, king of nations (Genesis 14)
5. None are mentioned by name

5,000

1. Jasper, sapphire, chalcedony, emerald, sardonyx, sardius, chrysolite, beryl, topaz, chrysoprasus, jacinth, amethyst (Revelation 21:19–20)
2. The bronze serpent Moses made in the wilderness (2 Kings 18:4)
3. The apostle John (Revelation 11:19)
4. Bezaleel and Aholiab (Exodus 31:1–11)
5. Jeduthun (1 Chronicles 25:3)

Other Trivia Books from
Barbour Publishing

Bible Marvels, Oddities, and Shockers
Paul Kent
256 pages.
978-1-59789-124-0

Fun Facts About the Bible
Robyn Martins
256 pages.
978-1-55748-897-8

Test Your Bible Knowledge
Carl S. Shoup
224 pages.
1-55748-541-0